PEOPLE MUST KNOW THE TRUTH

Jean Herbert Bradley

ARTHUR H. STOCKWELL LTD
Torrs Park, Ilfracombe, Devon, EX34 8BA
Established 1898
www.ahstockwell.co.uk

DEDICATION

I dedicate this book to John, my husband,
to Nicholas, my son, and to my beautiful daughter, Caroline.
Also to Lady Hazel and Lady Judith.

ISBN 978-0-7223-4801-7
Printed in Great Britain by
Arthur H. Stockwell Ltd
Torrs Park   Ilfracombe
Devon EX34 8BA

AUTHOR'S NOTE

After the children were grown and I became a mature B.Ed student, studying the history of art at Leicester University, I was encouraged by two devoted tutors to think beyond accepted boundaries and to consider all matters extraterrestrial as we deviated from science and history. I thank Mr D. Smith and Mr J. Finn (deceased) for opening my eyes to the known and unknown universe.

INTRODUCTION

From the beginning, in 1947, when Kenneth Arnold saw nine discs that he called flying saucers, humans have been intrigued by the phenomena of extraterrestrials and the subject has been taken seriously by many governments worldwide. Millions of sightings cannot all be imagination. How strange, then, that it was not until 1978 that the 1947 Roswell incident became public knowledge! Budd Hopkins, the world expert on abductions, has documented cases that are convincing from all over the known world.

However, do the aliens come from outer space or, as French astronomer Jacques Vallée believes, from parallel dimensions? This belief is getting ever more common among scientists who adhere to the parallel-dimension theories. In this book I examine the work of experts and the accounts of ordinary people and give my own interpretation.

After my own corroborated loss of time, I became a dedicated vegetarian and a more accomplished artist and developed an interest in divining, archaeology, geology and crystals. I can testify that Rugby is definitely a hot spot of UFO sightings, as this book reveals.

Conspiracy theories have existed since 1953, when President Dwight D. Eisenhower showed an interest in an RAF reconnaissance over Germany during which a strange craft was intercepted. When declassified papers became known it seemed that Sir Winston Churchill might have ordered this incident to be hidden for fifty years.

In the summer of 1994, my husband and I lost time travelling on the A5 near Rugby (see Chapter Seven). Another shared experience took place while we were driving near Kilsby, Warwickshire, one sunny summer afternoon. Suddenly we were in darkness and above us was a triangular craft. The undercarriage was smooth and black with no markings. This lasted only seconds before it rose silently and shot off over the fields. The size can be estimated if you imagine that it spanned the hedges on both sides of the road. My husband tried to remember as much as possible when we rushed home to write it all down. Nothing appeared in the local newspapers.

CONTENTS

CHAPTER ONE

ANTHROPOMORPHIC

In February 1968, the *National Enquirer* stated, to the amazement of the known world, that a leprechaun had been found. The mummified skeleton when X-rayed proved beyond doubt that it was sixty-five years old at the time of death. The tiny skeleton weighed only twelve ounces and was fourteen inches tall.

In 1932 in Wyoming, USA, a mummified man was discovered. He was fourteen inches tall. Nearby were found many vibrating discs. These, when struck, gave off different notes, almost musical.

In 1965 in Southern Ireland the earliest mummy found was at Cashel, Tipperary, and this had several discs beside the body. Each disc made a different sound and vibrated. When placed in sand the low-frequency vibrations caused a single circle to appear. High frequencies caused concentric rings around a centre circle

In 1923 in South Africa at Koffiefontein in the Orange Free State, south of Kimberley, graves only about three feet under the ground were revealed. These contained skeletons that were proved to be 10,000 years old. Arsenic and cobalt had been mined very near and this has been proven to affect silver. Were the little men protecting their claim?

In Mongolia men's skeletons were discovered which were fourteen inches tall. Investigations showed that they definitely were not foetuses, but were sixty-five years old at the time of their burial.

In 1956 in Londonderry (Derry) Mr Thomas Hutchinson saw a tiny pilot get out of a UFO that had briefly landed in his farm field. It makes one wonder if these skeletons are indeed extraterrestrial.

In 1938 in East Asia, 716 metallic discs were discovered in a cave in a mountain. When struck, each vibrated at a different frequency, and each gave off a different tone that could easily be identified. These stone discs were electrically charged, and a form of magnetism was suspected. Most of the weight was made up of cobalt (atomic weight, 5.90). Could this be a musical message from the stars? The skeletal remains that were found with these discs could not be ethnologically classified. Human or humanoid? The very high craniums were unlike earthly skulls. Could they have been part of a bizarre experiment that went horribly wrong? Cobalt was found near to several of the skeletal remains. Cobalt was named after the German word *Kobalt*, meaning demon, goblin or gnome, because nearly always there is a smell of sulphur or arsenic nearby.

In 1919 Charles Fort, an American writer, believed that tiny extraterrestrials had visited Earth. He had many supporters. (Read *The Complete Books of Charles Fort*, published in New York, 1974.)

In 1630 on Lewis in the Outer Hebrides, Scotland, very small skeletons were found along with skulls of unknown origin. After careful analysis these were declared to be not of human origin.

In 1836 when seventeen tiny coffins were discovered by boys out rabbiting at Arthur's Seat, Scotland, they caused a puzzle. The wooden bodies were wearing one-piece suits and moon boots. The Edinburgh museum confirmed that they were not wearing their original clothes. Mrs C. Couper, Tyron Manse, Thornhill, Dumfriesshire, donated them. Could they be facsimiles of the original bodies?

In 1976 Dr Walter Havernick, director of the Museum of Hamburgische Geschichte, wrote of a discovery in Saxony, now Westphalia, between the Rhine and the Elbe in North Germany. Tiny coffins were found and one body was described in the *Journal of Natural History*, page 66, as having a skull like a malformed rabbit skull. Maybe this was not a rabbit skull, but part of an alien?

Six coffins found in Germany in 1710 were not all made of wood like the Scottish ones; some were made of thin sheets of metal. What the metal was is not described in the literature. These, however, differed from the others as an animal skull was in the metal coffins with a wooden body. What kind of animal is not clear, but it must have been small to represent the head of the occupant of the small coffin – a mouse or vole or alien? The finders of the coffins speculated that it must be animal as it was not human – they would not have connected it with anything alien at that early date. When an abductee is describing an alien Grey they almost always describe a creature devoid of sexual orientation, and the occupants of these coffins had no sexual organs. This was what led me to my theory that the occupants found could be facsimiles of the former occupants. Anyone who used an animal skull as part of a child's toy would have to be strange indeed.

If it is true that the bodies in Germany were not found in coffins but were buried in the earth, it suggests that someone in Scotland may have given the remains found a Christian burial. The skeletons found in Ireland, South Africa and in Germany were, it is alleged, about twenty inches taller than the Scottish ones in the coffins, but there could still be a connection. If the finds in Scotland were originally found in a deteriorated state then maybe they were copied much smaller than the originals?

One very interesting fact to come out of all this is that in the sale catalogue in Scotland the finds were described as being natural-history specimens, curiosities and ethnological material. Not, as one would have expected, described as small carved wooden figures enclosed in wooden coffins.

Theories as to the origins of the tiny coffins:

1. That witchcraft practice may have required the occupants to represent real people.
2. They contained effigies of loved ones who were buried or died overseas.
3. They contained effigies of Scottish sailors lost at sea.
4. They were made by a deranged person obsessed with death.
5. Supernatural spirits lived in the coffins to bring good or bad luck.
6. They contained effigies of the original occupants, whose bones had deteriorated.

Were the vibrating stones found with the skeletons left here for a purpose, perhaps to guide or transport the extraterrestrial into another dimension or back to their home world? We can only guess at the present time and may never get the full answer. However, it is not difficult to believe that some sort of magnetism is at work when circles appear in sand and water when different sounds, vibrations and frequencies are applied.

A document at the Royal and Irish Academy, Dublin, Ireland, may show (it is alleged) that an ancient medical treatise written by fairies was given to a Connemara man whom they had previously transported to their lands.

Many people are reputed to have seen this document in the past. Whether it is still at the museum I cannot say.

Is there a connection between little people and UFOs? Read *The Humanoids*, published by Charles Bowen, 1969.

Read *Flying Saucer Occupants*, by C. and J. Lorenzen, published 1967. In this book over fifty sightings are recorded.

Read *The Unidentified*, by Clark and Coleman, published 1975.

In the Museum of Antiquities, Edinburgh, Scotland, on display you will find many 'fairy coffins' that contain wooden dolls. Their dress is not old, but gives the impression of being a copy of a spacesuit with moon boots. The intriguing thing is this, what did they contain before the boys who found them destroyed some of the evidence? Until they were eventually disturbed by these schoolchildren were the bodies only skeletons resembling animals and were they thrown away in disgust by the finders to be replaced with wooden effigies?

On 20 August 1965 in Peru, Alberto Ugarter and two friends saw a UFO land on some Inca ruins. Small people emerged from a saucer that was only five feet in diameter.

On Lewis, in the Outer Hebrides, in the sixteenth century it is believed that the Reverend Dean Monro found very small skeletons that were declared not human in origin. In 1630 a Mr John Dymes examined these bones and declared that their structure was such that they were definitely not human.

In his book *Archaic England*, Harold Bayley states that under Africa there are allegedly vast tunnels, part natural and part artificial, which gives rise to the Hollow Earth Theory. 'It took a caravan from sunrise to sunset to pass through one such tunnel,' it is alleged. Is it possible to believe that archaeologists have in the past suppressed evidence of such tunnels to quash the theory of under-earth dwellers?

There are tunnels under and through the Andes mountains, some natural and others artificial. Read *Secrets of the Ages* by ufologist Brinsley le Poer Trench about inter-terrestrials.

The British Museum has a bowl made of clay that portrays the figure of a creature which is neither human nor humanoid. The Hopi tribe of Native Americans made this clay pot, which shows a figure not unlike the ones depicted on the Mappa Mundi, an ancient map held at the cathedral in Hereford, which shows them around its margins. Reliable witnesses in ancient seafaring expeditions saw the monsters, sciapods and other non-humans. The body of the creature painted on the pot has no head, but a flap-like covering. The eyes are where the nipples would normally be. The legs are correctly positioned as if on a human. It has a slanted mouth under the eyes. This is almost identical to a creature depicted on the Mappa Mundi. Whether the drawings are imaginary or pictorial evidence we cannot be sure. They do, however, show that somewhere there could actually be people with only one leg and three eyes – people who still populate the forgotten places on this earth. Another explanation could be that they were aliens, actually seen while visiting this planet from outer space. The word 'extraterrestrial' comes to mind when people from opposite sides of the Earth draw and paint, for posterity, creatures that have no place in our world. Something gave them the foresight to record what was seen.

The *Chronicon de Melrose* (1065) describes strange beings: 'These one-legged humanoids left no discernible tracks.'

On 2 July 1947 Major Philip Corso saw a dead alien.

In 1961, fourteen years later, Lieutenant Colonel Philip Corso was working for the US Army in the Research and Development Division. He was assigned to report on an unusual matter – namely, what exactly were the contents of a number of wooden crates? Roughly thirty wooden crates were to be examined and their contents analysed. These were the same crates that had contained the dead alien bodies. Although no bodies remained, there were artefacts – material with writing on it and glass fragments reminding him of electrical circuitry. Also, to his amazement, there were fragments of aluminium that could bend exactly as the farmer, Brazel, at Roswell had described them. After intimidation Brazel had given back the pieces of metal to the air-force officers. Incidentally, his son confirmed this on his tour in 2007.

He also witnessed three small alien bodies in 1953 at Wright Patterson airbase, Drayton, in crates with wreckage from the Arizona Desert containing dry ice. Dr F. Hauser described the tiny bodies as human-like but hairless. Suggestions were made that their insect-like skeletons would have a very low body mass and therefore G forces would have very little effect on them.

In 1980 Puerto Rican Professor Calixto Pérez saw a dead humanoid in the caves at Tetas de Cayey. Jose Zayas killed the creature, but a photograph was taken and may be held by NASA.

Two Mirage F11 jets downed a UFO in the Kalahari Desert using Thor 2 laser cannons, which struck the UFO and caused it to crash, reported Captain J. van Greunen, who contacted Tony Dodd of *Quest* magazine to report the incident. Captain Greunen was a special intelligence officer in the South African Air Force at the time of the incident. High radiation readings surrounded the site and the craft. A silver disc was taken to Valhalla base for further investigation. When the UFO was housed in a hangar two creatures emerged from the saucer; they were less than four feet tall. Their grey skin was shiny and their large black eyes almost covered the whole surface of their faces. They were flown to Wright Patterson airbase.

Has evidence of intelligent early man been hidden? We are educated to believe that 4 million years ago bipedal hominids roamed our Earth. Has the truth been covered up because not 4 million but 8 million years ago humans and non-humans lived here on Earth? All the great libraries of the world have been destroyed, and so I ask the question Could Homo sapiens be an experiment? Humans, we believe, have evolved from the caves to the world of cyberspace in just a few years. How long before we stumble on the real origins of man?

The discovery of tiny skeletons could hold the answer.

CHAPTER TWO

GEOGRAPHICAL

In 1969 Jimmy Carter, president of the United States of America, witnessed a UFO incident, it is alleged. The sighting occurred on 6 January at Leary, Georgia, at 7.15 p.m., when he was the governor of that state. (From the *National Enquirer*, 8 June 1976.)

It is alleged that he said, "I am convinced that UFOs exist because I have seen one. . . . Twenty people saw it. . . . It was the damnedest thing I have ever seen . . . size of the moon . . . watched for ten minutes."

President Carter's military service was in the US Navy. Therefore he would have witnessed many strange things before this. His scientific training was in nuclear physics; this makes his testimony all the more believable.

In 1948 Lieutenant George F. Gorman chased a UFO over Fargo, North Dakota, USA, witnessed by traffic controllers Lloyd D. Jenson and H. E. Johnson. This was also seen by the pilot of a Piper Cub and corroborated by his passenger. (From *The Encyclopaedia of UFOs*, edited by R. D. Story.)

According to the late Dr J. Hynek, an astronomer writing in *UFO Magazine* edited by the late Graham W. Birdsall, when he was the scientific consultant to Project Blue Book and CUFOS he witnessed classified documents that are to remain classified for the foreseeable future – possibly for 100 years.

The official classifications of UFO sightings remain today as:

1. UFO seen at a distance of 500 feet.

2. UFO seen at a distance of less than 500 feet (CE1).

3. Car ignition and lights suddenly not working for no reason (CE2).

4. UFO seen with occupants (CE3).

5. Contact with aliens or abductions (CE4).

It is alleged that there is a big secret that has been kept from the human race for generations. Albert Bender was, in 1953, the director of the International Flying Bureau, Connecticut, USA. It is alleged that he was subjected to several 'interviews' by men in black, MIBs. He revealed his belief that there are extraterrestrial bases in Antarctica and was warned not to disclose his information.

His big secret was not disclosed, but it is believed that genetic engineering brought about the human race. Extraterrestrials once planned to inhabit Earth when their water became contaminated or evaporated.

Admiral Richard Byrd allegedly told President Truman, at the Pentagon, that on 19 February 1947 an expedition flew over the South Pole and recorded that they had seen a green valley with several lakes. They were buzzed by low-flying aircraft, seeming to fly at the speed of sound with Nazi markings on them. Their eight-month manoeuvres were reduced to a few weeks and 5,000 troops were kept in reserve in case they were needed. This reported incident appeared in several South American newspapers at the time.

In February 1947 a US Navy pilot, Lieutenant Commander Bunger, flying near to the coast of Queen Mary Land and Wilkes Land also saw an ice-free region with lakes of seemingly warm water.

Robert Morning Sky, a Native American, tells the interesting story that his grandfather and five other Indians nursed a 'Star Elder' back to health after the spacecraft that he was travelling in crashed in the US. The actual date was the exact day the Roswell incident took place. It is alleged that the 'Starman' told the Native Americans that the secret that had to be kept forever was that humans were genetically engineered under the scrutiny of their alien makers.

On 6 October 1977 *The Times* newspaper reported that 'Some lakes have been found under the Antarctic ice.' The discovery had been made by Dr G. K. A. Oswald and Dr de Q. Robin of the Scott Polar Research Institute.

In April 2003, in *UFO Magazine*, Dr Richard Saunders, PhD, wrote of archival evidence. The general public has not been told, claimed Graham Hancock and Michael Cremo, that in remote antiquity other civilisations may have inhabited the Earth.

May I suggest that maybe Antarctica was inhabited millions of years ago, and with careful exploration remains of civilisations will be found? Fossil remains, when found, will prove this theory. Then the world's great libraries, such as Alexandria's library, will have been systematically destroyed for nothing. Although most of the alien evidence has been either hidden or destroyed, you cannot hide the truth forever. As the late Graham W. Birdsall once said, 'People must know the truth.'

When Bob Lazar reported on the existence of 'back-engineering' he gave his theory about the secrecy being partly due to the panic caused in America when *The*

War of the Worlds was broadcast on the radio. Whole towns were paralysed with fear when they thought that an alien invasion was imminent. Where better to hide, if extraterrestrials do inhabit the Earth, than under a sheet of ice where no human could exist or would want to?

During the National Security Agency conference at Laughlin, Nevada, in 2003 a member of the US armed forces was the source of a speech in which it was alleged that a JPL satellite had detected a gigantic dome at one end of Lake Vostok in Antarctica. Forty journalists were at the conference, but the speaker was ushered away before the completion of her talk. Not long after this conference, two Australian women skiers ventured too near to the alleged installation and were removed, it was reported, by US Navy Seals for their own safety. The navy helicopter flew them to New Zealand. It was reported also that the Australian Government lodged an official protest to the USA.

What is hidden in Antarctica – an extraterrestrial base, a secret man-made installation or ancient civilisation secrets? Whatever it is has been kept hidden from the world at large. This suggests something sinister.

In April 2003 the late Graham W. Birdsall was allegedly warned to 'watch my back'. (*UFO Magazine*, April 2003.) He stated that he had met two US Atomic Agency officials who had warned him against publication of a photograph of a nuclear generator being unloaded from a US supply vessel in Antarctica. The photo appeared in the November/December 1998 *UFO Magazine* alongside an article by Brazilian scientist and Antarctic researcher Rubens Junqueira Villela.

Andrew Pike, writing in *UFO Magazine*, 1998, mentioned two agencies – The British Antarctic Survey and the British National Space Centre's Exobiology Committee – that were established to study extraterrestrial life.

From 1994 to 1996 RRS *Bransfield* was the British Antarctic Survey's Royal Research Ship. There were two support vessels at the time. The other was the RRS *James Clark Ross*. A serving member of the crew claimed that a top-secret British base was bring constructed in Antarctica.

On returning, the crewman enquired, "What is the base Europa S8 for?"

The answer surprised him: "The base does not exist. Speak of it again and you go home with no references."

In 1988 a curious incident took place according to Sir Ranulph Fiennes, the British explorer. An unmarked helicopter appeared from nowhere, hovered and a voice called, "You have strayed off course." Fiennes realised that there was no official base near enough to have sent the helicopter to warn them. It could not have been carrying enough fuel to return to a known base. Fiennes and his team had indeed strayed off course.

In Torquay, Devon, in 2007, when my husband and myself ventured out to sea on a boat trip we travelled along the River Dart. After a short time we were instructed by the crew to look out for the underwater laboratories at sea, constructed and used to test drugs for medical purposes. We saw nothing below the waves, but it started people speculating as to the true purpose of these underwater structures. My conclusion was that perhaps the installations were a trial run for underwater bases in another place – maybe the Antarctic? Other travellers commented that aliens could be using them to live and hide beneath the waves. Much laughter ensued, but I began to think positively, 'What if extraterrestrials use a form of communication that can't be detected under the water?'

As no one is sure of the origin of Earth's magnetic field is it possible that the interest in Antarctica could be related to the theory that the magnetic poles will at some time reverse? This phenomenon is called the Brunhes-Matuyama reversal. When this occurs, whether naturally or engineered, the space–time continuum may be affected, and the next ice age will occur. Evidence that this reversal did in fact occur 78,000 years ago is based on iron found in lava rocks. These rocks contain a magnetic charge from the time they were solidified. There is a connection between the Earth's molten core and its magnetic field.

On 28 February 2007 deep below Switzerland scientists were constructing a project to 'look at other dimensions'. Newton hinted that there are many more dimensions to this universe. Nine levels or dimensions have been guessed at, and the giant 'converter' below Switzerland may give some of the answers eventually. When the results are known it should be possible to assume that other entities have been or are entering our galaxy through the many levels or dimensions.

It has been reported in several countries that the USA military, have put a D-notice on the very existence of electrogravitics. If gravity is the key to these experiments then it has been a closely guarded secret for many years. (From *UFO Magazine*.)

In 1968 two archaeologists, Manson Valentine and Dimitri Rebikoff, were diving for treasure in the Bahamas. They discovered a submerged city approximately 800 feet in length and twenty-five feet below the clear waters. The area covered approximately twenty-six square miles. The city walls were in places 2,000 feet long and it was estimated that twenty tons is the average weight of the stone blocks. A date of around 10,000 BC has been estimated for the city. Atlantis is not the only city to have vanished.

In Africa, artefacts have been discovered that are made of copper, and they are estimated to be 20,000 years old.

The artefacts have animal and humanoid pictures worked on them. Mummies in the same region were carbon-dated and to everybody's amazement appeared to be 10,000 years old. Given the age of the treasures found with them they may well be a great deal older.

In 1950 a strange story emerged from Socorro, New Mexico. Grady Barnett saw what he believed to be a UFO crash site. Small humanoid bodies were lying in the wreckage at Magdelena, near Socorro. Archaeologists were the first to see these bodies and then the military arrived and removed them. All personnel at the Wright Patterson airbase, where they were taken, were sworn to secrecy.

In 1996 in Brazil a farmer saw little men stealing his chickens, and at about the same time in France the same thing was happening to another farmer.

On 24 April 1964 Gary T. Wilcox from Tioga County, New York, saw two small creatures that he called dwarfs stealing fertiliser from his farm. The humanoids told him that they were from Mars and would return eventually.

On 23 July 1947 Jose Higgins and his survey team in the USA fled from an extraterrestrial wearing what looked like a rubber spacesuit. What happened next was not reported.

In 1361 in Japan there was a report that a sea craft emerged from the ocean. It was twenty feet in diameter. (From the book *Passport to Magnolia,* by J. Vallée).

On 4 November 1322 in England at Uxbridge beams of light burst forth from the sky. This was so unusual that it was reported in several people's diaries.

In 1387 in Northamptonshire and Leicestershire a round

barrel of flame was seen in the sky over much of the two counties.

In 1461 in France iron rods were seen one and a half times the size of the moon.

On 12 November 1799 in Hereford, England, a large ball of fire was seen by many people.

On 19 November 1799 at Huncoates in Lincolnshire the same ball of fire was seen again. There were many witnesses.

On 10 June 1931 Sir Francis Chichester allegedly witnessed a UFO while at sea.

On 24 June 1947 when Kenneth Arnold saw nine objects, five were also seen by Captain E. J. Smith at Washington, USA, and by Ralph Stevens in Idaho, USA. Later Ralph Steven saw another four UFOs. It seems likely that they were witnessing the same nine UFOs. (From *The Encyclopaedia of UFOs*, edited by Ronald D. Story.)

The Mayans, who worshipped a feathered god, began their calendar at 3113. Why? We may never know for sure, but the evidence of the feathered god points to the stars. They have another god posing as a serpent; this adds fuel to the reptilian theory of a god from the sky that may not have been altogether bird-like. Also why was it alleged that the skulls of the children of wealthy parents were wrapped so tightly so as to elongate their heads? Could it have been to hide an inherited deformity? This practice reminds one of the Egyptian pharaohs' headgear that resembled an elongated skull, though in a hot country it would have been more sensible to have a wide-brimmed hat to ward off the sun's heat. What did they have to hide? Could it be the same inbred genes resulting from a mating with cosmic visitors or the result of biological engineering?

In 1948 when Project Sign became first Grunge and then Project Blue Book, 12,600 sightings were reported in the eighteen years that records allegedly were kept. Seventy of these were or could have been genuine UFOs.

In July 1947 the Roswell incident took place. It was not until 1978 that nuclear physicist Stanton T. Friedman learned by chance of the UFO crash at Roswell, Nevada.

"You should talk to Jesse Marcel" was always the answer to his questions about UFOs.

Friedman was the first person to investigate the Roswell incident. It seemed that the locals had either forgotten about it or were no longer interested. It was Stanton Friedman who discovered that a farmer, Marcel, and his son had actually handled pieces of the UFO. All evidence had been taken to the Wright Patterson airbase by the military.

In 1996 in *UFO Magazine* the late editor, Graham W. Birdsall, stated that 'People must know the truth.' He met, in 1998, the attorney and investigator Ubirajara Rodrigues in Brasilia and it transpired that on 13 January 1996 a hovering UFO had followed several cars. Then on 20 January hundreds of witnesses saw a UFO overhead.

Also on the same day as the incident Senhor Marco Freitas heard barking dogs at the Jardian Park zoo at Varginha, Brazil. It was reported that he captured a strange creature not seen before in that part of the country and he put it into a strong crate. Three local girls witnessed his actions. Younger children threw stones at the creature and called it names on account of it being so ugly. Senhor Freitas's body was hurriedly buried immediately after being found dead, probably to hide the scratches or bites incurred during the capture of the creature.

At the University of Campinas (Unicamp) in São Paulo, Brazil, the body was examined in their laboratories. Other laboratories examined the body, including four underground laboratories, the Institute of Biology and the

Hospital das Clinicas. It was alleged that the Brazilian Air Force Technology Centre near Tamoios Highway, six kilometres from São Paulo, received, at their laboratories, pieces of metal from a crash site near to São Paulo. Whether there is a connection to the extraterrestrial creature is not known. At the forensic medicine department at Unicamp, Dr Bradan Palhares later denied that he had carried out an autopsy on the creature. He had obviously seen the creature at close quarters, as his response to a journalist was "Who can face the horrible creature for more than one minute, let alone carry out the autopsy?" The creature was sealed into a metal box and frozen until April 1996, when it was guarded night and day at the Samarais cemetery in São Paulo until burial.

Another creature was seen visiting the Jardian Park zoo by a Professor Terezingo Gallo Clepf. She saw it in the bushes hiding at the zoo. She had been investigating why so many animals at the zoo had died of an unidentified virus. Again no connection was at the time suggested.

Strangely on 13 January 1996, a week before the creature was seen at Varginha, a huge amount of military activity had been seen in the area. Trucks full of soldiers and other personnel carried debris from a field near to São Paulo. The Brazilian Air Force may have found the crash site near to the Tamoios Highway six miles away and had begun their search for the elusive Varginha creature. Something else was unusual: many people from the nearby town had smelt ammonia around that time. This is not unusual near to a crash site or at the graves of 'little people', where cobalt and arsenic are associated with extraterrestrials.

Ubirajara Rodrigues, the attorney and investigator, said, 'I wonder, could UFOs and their occupants emanate from a water-like environment?' Did he speculate an association with ammonia and the underworld, or was it the reptilian nature of the Varginha creature that fed his curiosity and imagination?

Where had the creature been hiding between 13 January

and its reappearance on 20 January? Had it (they) escaped from capture by the military, which may have held it when the military activity was witnessed near São Paulo?

Dr Roger Leir, writing in *UFO Magazine* on 20 January 1996, listed the Varginha creature's characteristics.

Human-like entity.
Two figures seen, suspect a third.
Large head, large red eyes.
Compound fracture of leg.
Hand, four fingers; feet, three toes and claws.
Five feet tall with brown reptilian skin.
Strong bone: with osteoarthritis that healed itself in twenty-four hours.
Blood has more platelet cells than humans have.
Varicose veins.
Telepathically intelligent.

Some physical evidence was left after burial at the Samarais cemetery in São Paulo. The creature had been kept frozen in a metal box until April 1996, when a date for interment was decided, probably by the military.

In 1555 Archbishop Olaus Magnus, Archbishop of Uppsala in Scandinavia conducted a serious study concerning the sightings of a dragon-like creature with a scaly body and shiny eyes. It was a definite reptilian.

In 1755 the Bishop of Bergen, Erik Pontoppidan, saw and recorded his sightings of what he named a kraken. This creature emerged from the sea and rose high above the waves. This also was covered in scales, as one would expect from a sea creature. It was the creature's enormous size that was remarkable enough to be recorded.

In 2001 in Dingle Harbour, Ballymore, Ireland, at 5 p.m. on 4 February Lucinda Cooke and two friends saw what they described as a UFO. This craft shot out of the water three times and disappeared into the water again. This was witnessed in daylight and they alerted the coastguard. What happened next was not recorded.

On 8 July 1947 in Kerry, Ireland, lights were seen all over the Spa district although no actual sightings of UFOs were reported.

In 1990 lights appeared to a crowd of people in the Kenmore area of Ireland.

On 19 June 2002 Andy Flemming, a Reuters reporter in Australia, spoke to *UFO Magazine* about a reported incident in Beijing, China. It transpired that nine scientists were investigating a mysterious pyramid-shaped tower in China. The tower is fifty to sixty metres tall, and legend says it was used to launch spaceships. The western province of Qinghai's newsagency, the Xinham, reported that this structure on Mount Baigong has three caves with triangular entrances filled with red pipes that lead into the mountain. Unusual-shaped stones are scattered outside the entrances. So far there is no date to age the caves, but investigation is continuing. A research fellow studying social sciences at the Chinese Academy is reported as saying that extraterrestrial activity is worth looking into. The ratio of height to perimeter of this pyramid equals the ratio of the Earth's radius to its circumference. Is this a coincidence?

In 1994 H. H. Housdorf, a German archaeologist, visited China, where he saw many such pyramids. In a seventy-mile radius of Xion he allegedly saw 1,000 of these structures.

On the Tibetan border with China hundreds of large stone discs, thousands of years old, were found and no explanation as to their use has yet been established. Could their original use have been the same as the ones found in Ireland and South Africa? The report does not mention that they resonate when struck, as the other finds do. There are Tibetan legends that humanoid creatures helped the Earth to advance its knowledge in the remote past.

In Egypt below the paws of the Great Sphinx there appear to be vast chambers yet to be explored. The Egyptian Government does not sanction investigations and excavations at the present time. Electronic detectors used by archaeologists located these caverns.

In the Indus Valley, India, it is reported that artefacts of immense importance have been found and are being kept virtually secret until archaeologists investigate further.

In Sumer, Iraq, two distinct communities were living at the same time, but seemingly in different time continuums. One had a poor living from the land, while the other grew to be a world leader in many fields of knowledge. The two communities were only 500 miles apart, but one community appears to have lived in mud huts and spent their days working the land as farmers; the other people, living at the same time, had (it is believed) been given gifts from the gods. These gifts included advice on irrigation, writing, bronze working, astrology and maths.

In Colorado, the Navajo Native Americans believe that the bird gods brought them wisdom from the stars using 'sky ropes'. Could this legend originate in a collective memory of seeing spaceships and not being able to comprehend what they were? After all, the only things that flew at that time were bats and birds, and their bird gods would not have looked anything like spacemen as we know them. In their world the only thing used to climb would have been a rope; therefore anything that ascended or descended would have been naturally described as using ropes or rope ladders. When a shaman goes into a trance he receives wisdom from the gods – this is never disputed by the tribe.

In Utah, Native Americans drew petroglyphs of people ascending into and descending from the sky. This 'memory' had to come from somewhere, but flight as we know it had not been achieved by mankind at that time.

In Ohio there is a 400-metre-long depiction of a snake or reptilian biting an egg. What purpose did this serve? Was it a memory or an invitation to a god to return?

In the Sahara, Africa, giant men in spacesuits were drawn around 7,000 years ago. These cave pictures may not be accurately dated, but something was seen all those years ago that could not be explained and the occurrence was recorded. Or did visitors from space or from the future leave their graffiti for future explorers to discover? There are so many unanswered questions, and we can only guess at the answers. (See Chapter Three: Alien Art.)

The Dogon tribe in Africa know a great deal about the Sirius star system. They know that Sirius has a twin star that is hidden behind Sirius, even though that star is not visible from Earth. This seems impossible. When asked about their knowledge they reply that it was passed down from their ancestors, who were visited by 'star people'.

When Egypt was visited by J. A. Ulrich, a German engineer, he discovered models that looked like aeroplanes at a burial sight at Saqqara. They resembled F102 fighter planes. Did human time travellers from the future leave these to prove that their visit had taken place? Or are they a present from space travellers to tease and intrigue future generations? These artefacts can be seen in the museum in Cairo, Egypt. If the artefacts are a warning from extraterrestrials that they intend to return to the Earth, then maybe the visitors are reptilian. Water is a scarce commodity in our galaxy, and the Earth with its vast oceans could be just what the aliens are looking for to make a new home.

Below Ecuador there are caves and tunnels containing paintings and gold artefacts that depict serpents, flying reptiles and pyramids. Even if the reptiles can be explained away as pterodactyls and the serpents as dinosaurs that leaves the pyramids to be explained. Is it possible that extraterrestrials built pyramids yet to be discovered in Ecuador? Or were they disturbed before they could start the building work?

We know of the reversal of the Earth's polarity and of the Ice Age. Either of these two events may have disturbed the balance of nature to such an extent that the extraterrestrials abandoned their project. Advanced aliens would have understood the signs and acted accordingly, hoping to return in the future. Von Daniken tells us that almost the exact same artefacts were found in Peru, in his book *Gold of the Gods*. Coincidence? Well, maybe, but travel between the two countries was an impossibility around 20,000 years ago, so it seems unlikely that they copied one another. As carbon dating is not too accurate this means that these artefacts could have been made long before this date. How could this have come about when the only tools that have been found with the primitive people of this period were made of stone, such as flint. This seems to be proof that the indigenous people did not make the artefacts by themselves without outside help.

At Tiwanaku, Bolivia, 100,000 years ago, the natives knew about metalwork, soldering, smelting, silver work and even a primitive kind of electricity. There has been found evidence of all this that dates back to that time.

At Uluru, Australia, the Aboriginal tribes talk of the Dreamtime and the Earth energies brought by the 'Sky-People'. It is possible that their collective memories have been passed down through the ages and only a fragment of this great intelligence is remembered. Could the Earth energies be magnetism and gravity, both forces of immense importance?

At San Freudians, Luca, a serpent swallowing an egg is depicted in an illustration along with a dragon and a flying fish. This is the good-luck symbol for their ships and fishing boats.

The Indian deity Vishnu has been depicted as the celestial fish-man with scales.

At Mulhouse, Alsace, St Steven is depicted with a whale or a submarine. And what of Jonah – was his great fish a submersible craft? After all, we are instructed that his father was the Angel Gabriel, who visited his mother while his earthly father, Lamesh (A-mit-tai), was away at sea.

Gilgamesh of the Babylonians was seen in ancient paintings dressed in a reptilian or fish-like headdress with the body of a fish slung behind his back.

The Angel Gabriel, who appears in the Holy Bible and in the Koran, is seen to have feathered wings. This is not surprising as it appears that only Ezekiel has seen spaceships, and how else could it be shown that someone has come down from the sky but by giving him wings like the birds?

In Africa there is a god called Tororut who is depicted as having wings and originates from the stars.

At San Michele in Pavia there is a window showing a bi-tailed mermaid and there is wide speculation as to why she was venerated. Could she be a reptilian extraterrestrial?

Notre Dame in Paris has a stained-glass window with a snake and a crow painted on to it. What was the reasoning behind this? Could it be a reptilian with wings representing good over evil? Could it be something to do with the snake or serpent drawn on the staff of a doctor or healer?

In medieval times a serpent was often carved below the waterline in a church font that was used for christenings. The significance of this has been lost in the mists of time; we can only surmise the true meaning.

In Cuba remote ancestors built pyramids in underwater cities that measure seven miles square. This may not be another Atlantis, but adds fuel to the legend.

Forty miles off the coast of Gujarat in India several Palaeolithic underwater cities have been discovered. They range from six miles long to much smaller settlements. Dr S. Kathiroli, director of the NOIT, uncovered temples and streets. Pottery shards, carvings, jewellery, beads, human teeth and human bones were dated to 4500 BC. Graham Hancock confirmed this and said that the buildings were three storeys high and walls could be seen 400 feet in length. They also found artefacts from around 9000 BC. (From *UFO Magazine*.)

In 1738 Voltaire wrote a story called 'Micromegas', in which he stated that aliens had visited Earth. He was the first to write about extraterrestrials.

Jules Verne expected humans to visit aliens on their home worlds.

In *Gulliver's Travels* Jonathan Swift allows his traveller to visit other worlds through portals.

In 1658 Cyrano de Bergerac, in *L'Autre Monde*, wrote of a journey to the moon. There he meets beautiful humanoids that have tape recorders and rocket-propelled ships.

These preceded works by more modern writers who are said to have invented science fiction.

In 1638 Bishop Francis Goodwin wrote a story, 'Man in the Moone', in which he imagined swans flying his hero, Domingo Gonsales, to the moon in a wicker basket. He also guessed that tall humanoids would bring technology to the Earth.

In Egypt in the fifth-dynasty tomb of Ptah Hotep (5000 BC) at Saqqara there appears to be the head of an extraterrestrial at the bottom of a mural.

On the island of Svieques, Puerto Rico, the US navy was asked to leave because the islanders had seen a great object take water from the sea. They had also witnessed submersibles from below the sea flying into the sky and submerging again. Could these be extraterrestrials living in an underwater city, or are they amphibian and therefore can breathe under the water? Or they could be harvesting our water to be used on a dry planet or our moon before colonisation.

There are reports and tape recordings suggesting that astronauts did see structures on our moon. One such recording – "There are structures here" – was reported in *UFO Magazine*. Also it is reported that on the rim of a sand dune astronauts saw small humanoids, skinny, with long arms and egg-shaped heads with no discernible features. If they do exist then they would possibly need to harvest their water from somewhere near. It has long been proved that fuel can be made from the constituents of water, making this a valuable commodity.

In England there lies between Warminster, Stonehenge and Glastonbury a form of triangle said to be the Glastonbury Triangle. Thirteen ley lines have been found that lead to this part of the country. The knowledge to find these ley lines or the ability to build them came from some higher authority. Twigs shaped like a Y are used, or two metal rods, to aid divination following what must be lodestones under the earth. The mystery is this: were they there before man or have they been placed there since for a purpose?

Wherever we look there is undeniable evidence of aliens lending help to humans, but to what purpose? The eternal question is where did we originate and when?

CHAPTER THREE

ALIEN ART

There is evidence in medieval manuscripts and paintings that proves alien or extraterrestrial beings have influenced these works of art. One such painting depicting a red sky and a large bird giving birth to small grey creatures suggests a Martian atmosphere.

The *Glorification of the Eucharist*, painted in 1595 by Bonaventure Salimbeni, is displayed at the Church of San Lorenza Petro at Montalcino near Siena. This painting has a ball with antennae protruding from it in the foreground. This looks like a modern landmine or bomb made this century rather than something from the fourteenth century. Could this be proof that time travellers had visited and left proof of their visit or a gift from the extraterrestrials?

There is a painting showing hundreds of UFOs that were seen by crowds of people in 1566 in Basel, Switzerland.

On 14 April 1561 at Nuremberg, Germany, a pamphlet was written that tells of a great aerial battle over the town witnessed by thousands of local people.

In 1680 a gold medallion was struck to commemorate a momentous event when a great wheel was seen in the sky above France.

On 4 November 1697 two great wheels were seen in the sky above Hamburg in Germany. Many witnesses swore to this event.

From the fifteenth century, a painting of the Lippi school depicts a man looking up at a UFO. The artist is not named.

In 1452 Lorenzo Ghiberti painted *The Gates of Paradise*. On the right-hand side of the sacrifice of Noah on Mount Ararat a pyramid is clearly shown. Ghiberti's painting of the drunkenness of Noah also shows a pyramid among the animals.

In 1446 Paolo Uccello painted *The Deluge* to commemorate the flood and he also felt the urge to include a pyramid.

In Florence in 1359, after the Great Plague, pilgrims believed that the Virgin Mary and her angels came down and saved the city. Giotto painted what looks like spaceships above and around the Virgin Mary. Therefore it must be assumed that something extraordinary was seen in the sky to inspire his painting.

The Wilton Diptych, painted in 1395, shows the Virgin Mary with angel wings. This suggests that the Virgin Birth was indeed a gift from the God of the skies.

In Tuscany the Crucifixion procession carries paintings from 1271 that clearly indicate wings not only on the angels but also on the Virgin herself. Another astonishing fact is that the eyes of all of them are very big and dark, reminiscent of aliens.

The Francis of Assisi procession also carries icons and paintings from 1236 that may include hidden aliens. Other paintings in the Basilica of St Francis of Assisi show him with feathered wings.

Dominican and Franciscan monks claimed many miracles were seen in Florence, Tuscany, Italy, and in Vienna. They attributed these to gods from the skies, not just to the One God.

Paintings from the twelfth century usually show angels with wings descending from heaven. Why? No one thought this remarkable, but had blind faith that God resided in the heavens. No one questioned it, from the high-born to the lowly serfs.

In Padua, however, a small chapel houses a painting that clearly shows angels and reptiles.

Adam and Eve were tempted by a snake of some kind. Was this on Earth or elsewhere?

Ezekiel's angels, or aliens, all had four faces and flew in a great wheel. His description is so clear that he really must have witnessed them at first hand.

Angels reputedly took King Arthur of the Round Table to an island to be cured of his wounds. Where this island was located was not given. If angels are real then why not believe in the existence of extraterrestrials?

The Earls of D'Ottremonde in Belgium are reputed to own a book that shows a picture of Moses with the Tablets and a UFO in the painting.

In AD 776 at the siege of Sigiburg Castle in France many witnesses claimed on oath to have seen UFOs circling in the sky. The report is in a book called *Annales Laurissenses*, written in the eighth century.

Aert D. Gelder in 1710 painted *The Baptism of Christ*, which hangs in the Fitzwilliam Museum at Cambridge. There can be seen, if one studies the painting, hints of extraterrestrial activity carefully hidden from normal viewers.

In Egypt between 1778 and 1823 Giovanni Belzoni allegedly saw strange creatures on the tomb walls – not just the jackal- and bird-headed humanoids, but other combinations. Why would the ancient Egypians worship humanoid creatures if they had not actually encountered them? Could this be why ordinary people and lowly priests never entered the great temples? If these people were wearing false heads or masks then there is a possibility that they were hiding some sort of deformity. Modern thinking is that inbreeding was the cause of this, but inbreeding with whom?

In 1928 skeletons were found with heads enlarged out of all proportion to their bodies in a tin-mining area of Nigeria. Could these aliens have possibly been looking for cobalt?

In Kiev, Ukraine, prehistoric art painted with red ochre depicts an extraterrestrial with a large head and big black eyes. This is estimated to be 5,000 years old. Did the indigenous people witness an alien presence or did the alien leave this drawing as proof of his visit?

The cave paintings at Lascaux are said to be 17,000 years old, from the upper Palaeolithic period. The artist saw what he thought were creatures that had descended from the sky. To show this he gave some of these creatures beaks and others feathers. This would be a normal way to show that they had flown. (The Wright brothers were ridiculed as no one believed, at the time, that a craft heavier than air could ever fly.) At Lascaux the artist or shaman clearly drew spacesuits and helmets on the cave walls. Some of the caves have been closed to the public and tourists who are interested in ancient history visit caves with copies of the paintings. The official reason, I have read, is that many tourists touching the pictures have left traces of oil, etc., from their hands and this could ruin the artwork. Do we really believe that the copies are accurate in every detail?

Somewhere in Europe the oldest skull to have been found is believed to be 400,000 years old.

In Crete the Sun Temples were built for the worship of both the sun and reptiles. Paintings of priestesses worshipping both deities can be seen in the temples.

In 900 BC the Paracas culture in Peru, whose skulls were deformed and elongated, were thought to have used the binding method used in Japan on feet to squash the skulls of children while the bone was still soft. There is another line of thought that maybe this theory is a cover-up to disguise an inbuilt deformity that is a throwback from interbreeding and maybe extraterrestrial breeding.

Created between AD 100 and 700, the Nazca Lines seen from the air appear to include landing strips of some sort, and associated shards of pottery clearly depict figures with large heads and very big dark eyes.

An Aegean pottery figure from 3000 BC has eyes that are too large and arms that could possibly be used as wings.

The Minoan civilisation of ancient Crete worshipped goddesses associated with griffins, dolphins, snakes and saffron-gathering monkeys. Athletic priestesses would, at special ceremonies, grab a fully grown bull by the horns and leap on to the back of the creature. Scenes of these activities can be seen depicted on black-and-red pottery.

At Tikal, Guatemala, a stone was found with 800 different hieroglylphs carved into it. This is thought to be of Mayan origin. However, why would simple farmers need this much information? If their mathematics and astronomy came from the minds of a greater civilisation what became of them?

On Easter Island (Rapa Nui), where 900 statues stand five metres high, there is an unsolved mystery. When, on Easter Sunday 1722, Dutch explorer Jacob Roggeveen first saw these giant stone statues he was shocked. All he could find out from the natives was that 'birdmen' from the skies helped to build them and the force used was called 'Mana'. These Polynesian islands in the Pacific Ocean still keep the real secret; did extraterrestrials once visit these islands and leave proof of their journey from the skies?

When Giovanni Belzoni visited Egypt did he think that the blueprints for the pyramids could have been brought from the skies? Did he wonder how simple farmers gained the knowledge of mathematics, geometry and astronomy to build such accurate buildings? If, as many now believe, the aliens left some of their DNA in the ancestors of modern Egyptians then inbreeding would be essential so as to keep the gene pool pure and not lose their knowledge in future generations. This did in fact happen to the Romans, Greeks, Nubians, etc., who interbred with other tribes and lost their pure DNA forever.

CHAPTER FOUR

RELIGIOUS AND HISTORICAL

The Church of Rome executed astronomer Giordano Bruno in 1600; he was burnt alive for saying that other worlds may be inhabited.

The Jewish document Haggadah, according to Ufologist Dr Joe Lewels, contains a passage concerning Adam and Eve. This suggests that both Adam and Eve were covered in scales, but after they succumbed to sex their scales fell off. In several fifteenth-century works of art, the serpent is depicted standing on two legs and has a humanoid appearance.

In 1945 fragments of parchment were discovered in a clay pot. These became known as the Nag Hammadi texts. One sentence reads, 'Adam and Eve saw their nakedness they loathed their beastly form.' Does this mean that their punishment for sex was to lose forever their scaly form and be forever naked?

Above Secacah, in a cave, jars were discovered that contained not only religious texts but also protests against the Roman Empire, which was gathering momentum but could not be stopped. The province of Judea was becoming ever more violent when, in AD 68, Vespasian drove his legions through the Jordan Valley. The books of Isaiah and Joshua speak of the Sons of Light who fight Dark Forces, and John the Baptist also mentions Theudas, a strange Egyptian. Was Theudas the leader of the Sons of Light, and was he of human origin? Where he came from and what he achieved is not clear in the manuscripts. Was it he that suggested Gentle Jesus, instead of going along with the rebellion? How much more is there to be revealed and how much more is there hidden?

While fossil hunting I found my most precious fossil of the Cretaceous period – a tooth from an ichthyosaurus. This lizard-like dinosaur swam 65 million years ago on this Earth, and I have one of its teeth! Coincidence plays a part in all our lives and I feel that I was meant to find this tooth and to use my intelligence to try to unravel and then to reassemble the dinosaur reptilian jigsaw puzzle. There are so many seemingly unrelated pieces – the Bible, UFOs, reptilian reports and evidence in ancient artworks.

In Sicily, for example, it is believed that an amphibious monster called Pongo preyed on the people, terrorising all Christendom for many years. Eventually it was slain by the three sons of St George. There are said to be many ancient documents that relate this story. Pongo, it was said, was humanoid – partly human and partly reptilian.

In his book *Aliens: The Answer*, David Barclay wrote about humanoid dinosaurs that somehow wiped themselves out over 65 million years ago. Maybe some of these humanoids did survive and kept tiny mammals as their pets. The surviving and evolving dinosaurs could have developed intelligence far beyond our expectations. If the humanoid dinosaurs lived for 150 million years it is feasible that a great intelligence could have emerged. Did we become Homo sapiens and the dinosaurs the Greys? Why do the Greys wear black eye masks if they have nothing to hide? Are they wearing night sights only just discovered by humans? Do they conceal their true reptilian nature? That could be one reason that they do not suffer from G forces like human pilots. If the Greys, or extraterrestrials, have a skeleton as light as a bird or reptile then the G forces on their bodies would not be great.

Chinese aristocrats, we read, believe that they originate from dragons, the Indians believe that Nagas, one of their deities, is a serpent god, and the Dogon people of Mali believe that Nommo, their god, gave them extraordinary astrological knowledge. These seemingly simple people understand the planets, star systems and comets to a degree well above the normal civilised world. Some of the things that they understand cannot be seen from the Earth.

Why do we fear snakes? Why did St Patrick banish them from Ireland? How did Jonah survive in the stomach of the whale? Look to the Holy Bible for some of the answers. When Noah was born his earthly father, Lamech, had been away for many, many months, and his skin was as a snakeskin, not a match for his mother or brother; his hair was white (also at odds with the rest of his family). His great-grandfather, Enoch, told him that 'guardians of the sky' had seeded his mother. Noah's father had been told that Enoch had been 'up to heaven on a fiery chariot'. Therefore miracles can be said to 'run in their family'. Is it possible that Jonah was also a 'gift from the gods' and part reptilian? Then it is feasible that he could have breathed inside the whale? However, if the 'whale' were an underwater submersible of some kind then it would have been mistaken for a whale.

It is said that Rameses III (1198–1167 BC), who released the Israelites from bondage, came from heavenly seed. Rameses means 'the sun god bore me'. Why did Nefertiti (consort to Akhenaten) and Rameses II wear tall hats and not a wide-brimmed one to keep off the sun? Did they need to hide elongated heads – their legacy from ancestors, maybe aliens?

Angels have appeared throughout history, not only in the biblical texts but also in the Holy Koran. The Angel Gabriel appeared as the Muslim spirit of truth to the Prophet Mohammed. In a cave in the mountain of Hira, near Mecca, the visitation took place. The Prophet was taken to heaven and his coffin was suspended above Medina with no visible supports (Daniel 8:6–26).

An angel told Zechariah that he would have a son called John the Baptist (Luke 1:3 and 23).

The Angel Gabriel spoke to the Virgin Mary and said that she would bear Jesus.

Ezekiel saw wheels and angels and heard a rushing of water as the wheels turned. He saw clearly what he thought were people with four faces.

Jacob watched as angels ascended and descended a ladder up to heaven, and he described them as having wings to enable them to climb or fly into the sky.

A spirit, or an angel, opened St Paul's cell; this is believed worldwide.

Moses heard voices from the heavens when he saw the burning bush. Did he wonder where the voice originated or was his faith so strong that he trusted in the One God?

The story of the conversion of St Paul (Saul) tells us of a great light that flashed and blinded him when the voices came to guide him. Were these voices also angels or perhaps extraterrestrials? Maybe they are one and the same.

In Mexico the Quetzaccott people worshipped the feathered serpent. Was he angel, bird or space lizard?

The Incas and Aztecs dressed as feathered birds and also worshipped reptilians that came to them from the skies.

Egyptians worshipped a sacred bird god known as Horus. His head represented a bird while his body was humanoid.

Vikings believed that Valhalla was somewhere up in the skies.

A Native American tribe called the Yaki, who lived in the Pennine Hills, Washington state, are reputed to have seen lights in the sky before an earthquake. They worshipped a sacred bird god.

Before he defeated Athelstan, Achaius, King of Scotland, saw a great cross in the sky. He took this as a sign from heaven that he would win the battle.

All throughout history we can see the religious connections with serpents and birds. Holy books and works of art show us these connections, from primitive cave paintings to great works of art in cathedrals around the world.

On his march to Rome, Constantine saw a luminous cross in the sky the night before the Battle of Saka Ruba in AD 312. The voice from the sky called out, "Paint a cross on each shield and you will surely win the battle against all odds." Like so many before him, he did not question the word of God.

A spokesman for the Vatican has been quoted many times as saying, "Extraterrestrials exist and are our brothers." The Vatican has an interest in space and owns a massive telescope, which may be the largest in private ownership.

On Mount Ararat in Turkey artefacts dating back thousands of years have been found. Ararat is where remains of Noah's Ark are said to lie.

The Great Pyramid at Giza houses the tomb of Pharaoh Cheops; this may have been built around 2554 BC. How did primitive people, mostly farmers, gain their knowledge of the stars and the heavens? They appear to have known that the celestial pole is not fixed and drifts on a 25,000-year cycle. These ancient people located the pole between two stars – Kochab in the Little Bear (Ursa Minor) and Mizar in the Plough, looking north between the two. The Queen's Chamber shaft faces towards Canis Major, whose brightest star, the Dog Star, is associated with Isis. The King's Chamber is facing Thuban in the constellation of Draconis, the Dragon. The lowest of the three stars in Orion's belt is Zeta (Alnitak) and is associated with Osiris, god of resurrection and rebirth. Orion is called 'Bringer of the First People' in the ancient texts. Of course the god Horus is always depicted with a bird's head.

In Genesis chapter 5 we learn that Noah was the ninth generation from Adam; he was so perfect that he was chosen to procreate after the flood. He had found favour with God (Genesis 6:8). In Babylon there is a flood story almost parallel to this biblical version. Gilgamesh, the Mesopotamian hero who ruled Uruk in 3000 BC, told of searches for the Wise One who, it was said, was the only survivor of the flood of Babylon. Akkadian language tablets found at Nineveh in the Assyrian library that was built by King Ashurbanipal reveal this story.

Cuneiform writings from Sumeria in Iraq (Sumer) tell of a time when the river Euphrates was south of Nippur, in South Central Iraq. There, in a Sumerian city called Shuruppak, a great flood happened, and all died except Ziusudra and his family. A messenger from the heavenly gods had forewarned them to go to high ground and build a boat. The date was between 10,860 BC and 8700 BC.

There are, in India, Sanskrit writings that tell of Manu, the first King of India, who built a very large boat before a great flood as instructed by the gods.

In Mexico, the Aztec people told of two people who survived the great flood when the mountains disappeared in a deluge. They were Coxcoxtli and his wife, Xochiquetzal. They also had been forewarned by their gods and were deemed to be so perfect that they should procreate to populate the dry world that would follow the flood.

In South America the Brazilian Tupinamba people told stories of a great flood.

In Chile the Araucanian people also remembered a great flood in their stories.

In Ecuador, Canarian people remember a great flood in their tales, but they believe many people survived.

In California, the Luiseno Native Americans recall a great flood in their dances and rituals.

Also in North America, the Huron and Mohican Native Americans have legends about a great flood that happened in the times of their forefathers. They retell the stories in song and dance of how a holy man built a boat of enormous proportions and a few people were saved to breed when the floods receded.

In China, Ta Yu, founder of the Hsia dynasty, dispelled a great flood when the gods forewarned him.

The last ice age began around 15,000 BC and deglaciation lasted 7,000 years, when the oceans rose up to 400 feet. All animal life disappeared, but fossils dating from 9000 BC have been found. The big question is how did the Earth become populated again? Did help come from extraterrestrials, and have they returned at intervals to see if their investment came to fruition? What covering did Adam and Eve have before they saw their nakedness? Perhaps it was scales.

One common phenomenon that regularly occurs in my research is the appearance of sky battles. In Ireland in 1797 it was reported in a local newspaper that several witnesses saw sky battles. In this quote from *The Elder Faiths of Ireland* by W. G. Wood-Martin he relates that an army of small men (fairies) marched as an army near to Maryborough in Ireland in 1797. This was recorded as happening at noon in broad daylight.

At the Ballyfrian Hills in 1836 a similar vision was seen by hundreds of people.

A different army seems to have invaded Kilkenny in Ireland in 1800. This time the marauding groups of little people were a savage tribe no more than two feet in height. They left clear trails of blood that were seen by witnesses after the savage tribesmen left the vicinity. People of the time referred to them as fairy armies or leprechauns. John Wesley, the preacher, also believed in the reality of phantom armies, it is alleged in several books. He is said to have believed that either God sent them or the Devil did – he was never explicit.

There is in the British Library a pamphlet that records an incident that allegedly took place in Suffolk on 4 August 1642. 'Noises and signs so strange were seen in the sky, when a witness saw a stone fall from the sky on a clear day.'

About fifteen miles from my home town of Rugby, Warwickshire, at Kineton, on four successive Saturday and Sunday nights on the battlefield of Edgehill people saw, and swore to it, the re-enactment of the Battle of Edgehill. King Charles, who was living at Oxford at the time, sent messengers to see for themselves. He was so disturbed by these phenomena that he made his men make sworn statements that the battle did appear just as if it was again happening. This was of course before the Civil War Battle of Naseby in 1645.

On 23 June 1744 in the Lake District, England, there were tales of phantom armies up in the hills witnessed by whole villages of people.

In Ripley in Yorkshire, England, it was reported in the local newspapers that a whole army was seen in the sky on 12 October 1881. This information is from a Mrs Crowe in her book *The Night Side of Nature.*

Sometime in August 1914, the retreat from Mons in Belgium had begun when "We saw cavalry alongside us not wearing the same uniforms as was normal. They came so close to our horses that were pulling the heavy guns that they spooked the team and make them nervous. Some of me mates was so scared of the larger chargers that they began to sing hymns. When I hears the Non Nobis Dominae I shakes with fear at the memory of them there great horses and their cavalrymen wearing the wrong uniforms." The account comes from the memory of Gunner Walter Herbert, army number 116193, at no. 1 depot, RGA, Fort Burgoyne, Dover.

In Holland at Dordrecht on Friday 17 May 1552 hailstones fell from a 'foul-smelling cloud'. No one ever discovered where the cloud originated.

In November 1921 at Chico, California, USA, rocks and stones fell down from a clear blue sky when there were no clouds at all.

When Joshua led the Israelites, to chase the Amorite army down the Beth Horon mountain, down to Azekah, the Lord threw rocks to kill the Amorites (Joshua 10:10–14). Did the sun really remain motionless or was the shining object seen by the armies a mother ship?

According to Livy's *Roman History*, King Tullus (672–

640 BC) defeated the Sabines with the help of stones thrown from the heavens.

Sometime before 2500 BC twelve miles east of Giza, in the city of Heliopolis, the Temple of Phoenix housed an artefact made of stone called the Benben Stone. This name translated means 'procreation' or 'seed'. The people of the time named it the Temple of Phoenix because the stone flew from heaven like the mythical bird. This stone was worshipped as if it were sent from God. The nearest star to the Earth is Proxima Centauri and it is calculated as being 4.3 light years away. Quite a way for a stone that is not a meteorite to travel! One theory is that the stone originated on Mars. As Mars passes less than 30 million miles from Earth this is a possibility.

At Oxford University, England, in 1991, a Dr Clark Friend, a geologist, discovered a 'chemifossil' that he dated as being 3,850 million years old. Using an electron microprobe they were able to determine the approximate age of the rock.

In 1994 when Steve Mojzsis from Scripps Institution of Oceanography, Los Angeles, California, discovered an interesting rock that they named G91/26 this also proved to be a 'chemifossil'.

Bacteria found in rocks in Australia in the Apex Cherts are alleged to be 3,500 million years old. A mass spectrometer reveals graphite and carbon grains within the grains of apatite, calcium phosphate. This is found in teeth and bones and appears to be evidence for ancient life.

Professor Gustof Arrhenius of the University of California, San Diego, reputedly confirmed this when he said that "Carbon 12 is more than three per cent more abundant than expected if life were not present."

An important contribution to this discussion made, allegedly, by Steve Mojzsis is that 'Life could have come from Mars. This would be one solution to many problems. There is still extreme scepticism as to life on the rock ALH84001 confirmed by evidence of contamination or just another cover-up?

Ancient maps may give us some vital clues as to what extraterrestrials look like, especially the highly decorated Mappa Mundi.

CREATURES FROM THE MAPPA MUNDI

Ambari – have feet facing backwards.
Blemyes – have no head, eyes in chest.
Centaurs – half horse, half man.
Cicone – man with large beak.
Cigolopes – have a tail and webbed feet.
Dippopods – horse-footed men.
Dog-headed men.
Eurusnothus – have forked tongue protruding from one eye socket.
Gangines – very tall men.
Humanpodes – they walk on all fours.
Hermaphrodites – are both male and female at the same time.
Mandrakes – plant men who squeal when they are uprooted.
Martimi – have two sets of eyes.
Men with closed mouths but a hole in the stomach.
Phanesil – bat-eared men with ears that touch the ground.
Race with protruding long tongue to shield them from the sun.
Subsolonus – walks on its head with several feet protruding from the head.
Scinopeds – have one eye and only one leg.
Sptemtria – have head on backwards.
Satyrs – goat-headed men.

Troglodytes – wild men who live in caves.
Tigolpes – web-footed men.
Zosimas – men with no arms.

Before the Mappa Mundi there was the Cotton Tiberias map, which the Anglo-Saxon monks drew of the world between 1025 and 1050. This is the earliest map known to exist. Even this may be a copy of a Roman map made 1,000 years earlier. The east, represented by a rising sun, is always at the top of ancient maps. Jerusalem is always the centre of the map for religious reasons.

The Carta Marina, drawn by cartographer Olaus Magnus in 1539, describes monsters, a sea hog and scaly creatures.

CHANTER FIVE

RENDLESHAM FOREST

In East Anglia, east of Ipswich a great forest stretches across Suffolk to the coast near Sizewell. This is called Rendlesham Forest. There used to be NATO bases at Bentwaters and Woodbridge leased from the RAF, who decommissioned them for the use of US Air Force personnel, and the US National Security Agency was also housed there. (From *UFO Magazine*.)

On Christmas Day 1980, Gordon Levett, a local man, saw a UFO and on 26 December the same year the Webb family saw what they believed to be a UFO. They testified that it was not a Chinook or an A-10 Thunderbolt as they could recognise the shapes of these. The family was between Woodbridge and Orford when they saw the craft.

When Budd Parker and John Burroughs saw a light in the forest near RAF Woodbridge this was reported to their superiors, who began an investigation. US Air Force driver Herman Kavanasac and Sergeant Jim Penniston investigated the incident and they had a surprise. The object that had landed was the size of a tank and covered in alien markings. There was a force field around the craft and radiation had burnt the treetops as it crash-landed amongst them. The airmen could not get too close because of the strong force field. However, the MOD did not immediately investigate in the forest. It was not until the next night that Commander Ted Conrad and Lieutenant Colonel Charles Holt, USAF deputy base commander at RAF Woodbridge, investigated. Lieutenant Bruce England carried his tape recorder and Sergeant Nevells and John Burroughs' Geiger counter showed radioactivity present in the immediate area.

Researcher Brenda Butler is reported to have seen small extraterrestrials floating around the crashed UFO as if making repairs. She allegedly said that they had grey skins and very large dark eyes. (From *Sky Crash*, by Jenny Randles, Dot Street and Brenda Butler.)

The British Ministry of Defence on 13 January 1981 received the first memo from Lieutenant Colonel Charles Holt through the Freedom of Information Act. This allegedly described that he saw unexplained lights on 27 December 1980, and gives details of the landing-ground radiation recorded during the second sighting, on 26 December 1980.

Lieutenant Holt, who had served in Vietnam and was promoted to colonel, was not given to imagining things. Later he was to become commander of 81st Fighter-Bomber Wing at the Bentwaters base. Just before retiring in 1992 he was on the staff at the Pentagon. His second memo has not yet been released through the Freedom of Information Act for national-security reasons. This could be held for another 100 years.

There has been speculation that the radiation at Bentwaters caused a portal to open into another dimension, either by accident or design.

It was only after more than twenty years that the British Ministry of Defence released the classified papers to interested parties. These included Lord Hill-Norton, Georgina Bruni, Andy Roberts and Dr David Clarke of Sheffield University, England.

The memo states 'A glowing object 2–3 meters across, pulsing, hovering, disappeared, seen again after one hour near the back gate of a farm where the animals were in frenzy. Next day the beta-gamma readings were 0.1 milliroentgens at the floor of the crash sight.'

Later that night witnesses saw what appeared to be a red sun that broke up into five objects and then disappeared. Local investigators Brenda Butler and Dot Street reported a UFO incident and so did Ann Hopton-Scott. She is reported to have stated that bright lights whooshed over her car. Julia Abbot told how the object that she saw was oval-shaped with lights. Gerry Harris, another witness, said that it was Christmas time when the lights came up and down and forwards and backwards and voices were heard shouting from the base and air-force vehicles were rushing about. Gary Collins saw lights and a triangle that flew past him and into the forest.

To quote from the late Graham W. Birdsall, former editor of *UFO Magazine*, 'I agree with the comments made by the interviewees that until Lieutenant Colonel Charles I. Holt, USAF, finally reveals all that he knows, we cannot be completely sure that he is alone in his knowledge of what truly took place at the Rendlesham Forest.'

There has been a USAF base at Lakenhurst since 1956.

The following report is from the November issue of *UFO Magazine*: 'It can now be revealed, that the M.o.D. denied that the incident at Rendlesham forest was of major defence significance, but, now, they confirm that it was of major significance.'

Squadron Leader J. D. Badcock, Ops (GE), claimed that the base radar was switched off on the afternoon of 29 December 1980. All radar readings are recorded. The Southern Track Production Area is part RAF and part NATO and men and women from several different countries are stationed there.

A report allegedly from Watch Officer Budd Huran, from Texas, reads, 'Two types of primary air defence radar were in operation that day in 1980. Type 84 + 85 also height-finding radar HF 200. It has been suggested that simultaneous equipment going wrong at the same time smells fishy.'

Rumours of a UFO cover-up were rife in 1980–81.

A reliable witness on the base, Gary Baker, allegedly claimed that the Official Secrets Act had to be upheld. He was cautioned when the representative from the MOD allegedly removed all tapes of the incident and all the relevant radar information from the base.

If the speculation is true that a portal into a parallel world could exist, how many are there? Who knows where they are located? Why is the information kept secret?

CHAPTER SIX

REPTILIAN

Captain John Ridgeway and Sergeant Chay Blyth, in 1966, claimed to have seen a great sea serpent. The serpent was judged to be thirty-five feet long. After their ninety-two days at sea, Captain Ridgeway was reported to have said, "I am no longer a disbeliever." What exactly they saw we can't be sure. What is sure is that many eminent sailors have, through the ages, seen and witnessed strange creatures that cannot be found in natural history books.

Way back in 1200 it was reported in the *Chronicon Anglicanum* that when a merman was captured and tortured he gave nothing away as to his homeland. The chronicler, Ralph de Coggershall, relates that on the orders of King Henry II Lord Bartholomew de Glanvill carried out the investigation at Castle Orford.

Satellite images taken by the US Mapping Agency as recently as 2000 are reported to show that in the part of the Atlantic that we call the Bermuda Triangle there are islands that appear to float above the surface of the sea. There are shadows below the islands that could not appear if the islands were in the sea. One clear image shows a solid island several feet above clear water. We can only guess, but to me it does suggest perhaps a mother ship hovering and being mistaken for an island.

Aristotle in the fourth century saw serpents so large that they could have devoured oxen.

Our own St George, born in Coventry according to *The Little Book of Saints*, slew a dragon that was about to devour a maiden. England had the Dragon of Wantley, which was famous for its ferocity. Maybe these dragons could hide in the sea, like the crocodile; this would have made them land- and sea-going creatures.

Richard Carrington wrote of the mermaids seen by numerous sailors and of monsters of the deep that he called dragons and mastodons.

Greek mythology tells tales of Perseus, Andromeda and dragons.

At Hereford Cathedral in England, the Mappa Mundi has wondrous scenes of monsters. Where did these images come from – surely not from the imagination of simple seamen? For example the man with an eye on his stomach and no head – I believe that to a simple fisherman that would be unthinkable.

During their travels in 1493, Herodotus and Ctesia wrote of seeing a man with hooves like the god Pan, and of a man with just one very thick leg, and also one with only a central eye in his forehead. These could of course be cripples and hideously malformed normal humans, but there remains a doubt.

Marco Polo swore on oath that he had seen dog-headed men in India.

Dr Seth Shostak, writing in *UFO Magazine*, states, 'The Milky Way has 1.5 billion planets, many will have intelligent life.' He goes on to say, 'Our initial contact will most likely be with some kind of self-replicating machine.' He does not specify, animal, vegetable or mineral; therefore it need not necessarily be a robot as we imagine them.

Dr Seth Shostak also hints that on first contact we may see aliens the size of dogs with reptilian skin. He also states that they could have four arms, as this would be useful, and mouths in their stomachs to enable digestion to take place earlier. Maybe the Mappa Mundi should be studied more often and more carefully in case it contains vital clues to extraterrestrial life. Dr Shostak presumes that the extraterrestrials could be of all shapes and sizes, but probably small (about four feet tall). We accept the diverse shapes of zoo animals without question. More gravity in alien worlds would make a small stature more likely. Aliens could possibly have advanced technology that we have never dreamed of. Humans could be a source of food for them as we use cattle and sheep or, worse, we could all become their slaves.

The director of the Institute for the Search for Extraterrestrial Intelligence in California (SETI) used to be funded by NASA. Now Microsoft, Intel and Hewlett-Packard fund this important research. First contact may not be far away.

In Ohio, USA, there is a great mound dedicated to the serpent god. It stretches for miles and from the air it can be appreciated how long this structure must have taken to build. Something or someone created this to remind the people of a vision or visitation, lest they forget. A huge undertaking like this by primitive people must have had a purpose and a strong belief in who or what it commemorates.

The Teotihuacan people between 700 BC and 400 BC built a great temple to the feathered-serpent deity. They also built, around the same time, a pyramid dedicated to the sun and moon gods and a grand palace in which to worship the feathered butterfly. Is it possible that their ancestors saw a flying serpent or an angel and were so stunned by this apparition that they felt compelled to commemorate this with not only a temple and palace but with a pyramid also?

Why go to all the trouble to build these great structures unless they were to house and hide something that would be of use to future generations?

Even in the twenty-first century the true purpose of the Great Pyramid has not been revealed. Intelligent aliens or humans from the future have left little in the way of clues to help us decipher the riddle. As previously related, beneath the paws of the Great Sphinx there lies a chamber. It will be explored when the Egyptian Government gives permission, but until then investigation is not permitted; therefore the world must wait. Ancient Egyptians called the sphinx Hor-em-adhet, translated to 'Horus at the horizon'.

Horus, the child of Isis and Osiris, could also be called Hera, meaning 'face'.

The first people to see the coincidence of the sphinx and the face of Cydonia on Mars were Dr Lambert Dolphin of Stanford Research Institute and NASA consultant Richard Hoagland in 1983. They decided to investigate further. (*UFO Magazine*.)

When President Clinton kept his promise to send the Pathfinder probe to Mars, did he know that the jackal-headed god Upuaut translated means 'Pathfinder'?

The Voyager 2 spacecraft probed both Europa and Io and found evidence of liquid on both moons with seas on Europa being able to sustain life. It may be possible for a reptilian race to be living on Europa if it is true that the seas can sustain life.

It is unlikely that Jupiter could support life as the extreme temperatures are long-lasting due to its size. However, conditions on Europa and Io could sustain advanced life as they have oceans and the atmosphere has been there for millions of years.

"If there is life in the universe it is going to be on the moons orbiting 16 Cygni C and 47 Ursae Majoris B." (Darren Williams of Pennsylvania State University, USA, quoted in *Nature* magazine, 1997.

Medieval manuscripts show Babylonian seals that are at least 3,000 years old; this seems impossible without outside intervention.

The Benben Stone in the Cairo Museum, in Egypt, is made of diorite. It has two rows of hieroglyphs evoking the rising sun, Lord of the Horizon. This is alleged to be from the home of the deity Sahu, who resides with Osiris in the constellation of Orion. Osiris was believed by the Egyptians to have seeded the world.

Two shafts in the Great Pyramid at Giza point to Sirius in Canis Major and to the centre star in the belt of Orion. This is how the stars would have appeared in 10,500 BC. However, if humans were not on this earth at that time then who engineered the pyramid? And what lies beneath the sphinx?

The passing of time is sometimes represented as a snake, and in many cultures he is called Ouroboras. The circle formed by the snake is a symbol of space; therefore the snake or reptile is at once a symbol of time and space in a form understood by primitive people.

It has been suggested by Castello that an underground facility exists, and this secret underground base has seven sub-levels where research is carried out on hypnosis and telepathy. He estimates that as many as 18,000 Grey extraterrestrials work there and reptilian humanoids that are called Dracos.

The research carried out at these seven sub-levels also involves analysis of dreams. (From *The World's Greatest UFO Stories*.) Level six is alleged to be Nightmare Hall, where tanks containing mullet-armed and mullet-legged humans are housed. Cages hold humanoid bat-like creatures that are mute. Cold storage holds humanoid embryos, according to Castello. He is alleged to have witnessed humans in cages, drugged and crying for help. The staff called the people insane and he was instructed not to talk to them.

It is sometimes assumed that reptilians and Greys have been here on Earth for thousands of years. They seem to be interested not only in electro-gravity, but also to a greater extent in genetics. Modifications to the human race may be the preparation for organic genetic alteration of their people to enable them to live on Earth when their own planet disintegrates or runs out of essential commodities.

The Howard Hughes Medical Institute may have funded this bizarre research with the National Science Foundation and the National Institutes of Health along with the US Department of Energy. No one has yet claimed overall responsibility. These claims of course could be false, but secrets have a habit of escaping.

From 1976 to 1978 Dulce was the centre of cattle mutilations. In July 1978 scientist Howard Burgess discovered his cattle covered in strange marks that only appeared under ultraviolet light, and he remembered a lot of UFO activity in the vicinity. The government of the time denied the existence of a military installation in the area that could be connected with these bizarre mutilations.

It has been suggested that the cattle had been subjected to genetic experiments carried out by reptilian extraterrestrials, Greys or humans. Their purpose is unknown.

CHAPTER SEVEN

ABDUCTIONS, LOCAL AND NATIONWIDE

Travis Walton was snatched from the Apache Sitgreaves National Forest, near Heber, Arizona, USA.

There is a legend spoken of in the USA concerning the Jicarilla Apache and published in 1898 by J. A. F. L. 'When the Apache emerged from the underworld . . .'

Another legend, related in the book *Indians of Arizona*, published by Houghton, 1929, states that 'The first people (Apache) emerged from a cloud, in this cloud were lights like rainbows.'

In 1953 at Crick, a village in Northamptonshire, several villagers, all now sadly dead, witnessed a UFO on the A428, which runs from Crick into Rugby and passes the Rugby Radio Station. This transmitting station was dismantled in 2006, when all twelve masts were considered to be of no further use.

Kilsby Lane runs between the villages of Kilsby and Crick not far from the border of Warwickshire. Travelling along this lane, enjoying the lush green landscape, my husband, John, and I witnessed something that we will never forget.

All of a sudden the sky darkened and we were under a very large shadow. There was not a cloud in sight, but nonetheless a dark shadow covered the entire car. Looking up and in front of the car, we saw to our amazement an enormous black triangle not 100 metres above us moving slightly upwards at a steep angle. It was so wide that it almost touched the hedges on both sides of the road. No sound was emitted from the craft, but a sort of vapour trail came from the back or under the triangular shape. I thought it was about to crash into the field on my left, but it hovered with the underside towards us. There were no markings that I remember; I think it was smooth underneath. We (my husband and I) had our photograph taken under the Concorde before we flew in it, and that had an undercarriage, but I saw on the triangle only a smooth surface. I cursed the fact that we did not have a camera with us to record this unusual incident. After a couple of seconds it shot almost vertically into the clear sky and as there were no clouds we could see it clearly as it shot away at an incredible speed. From hovering to disappearing took only seconds and we wondered what we had seen.

Arriving home, I wrote down a description and John verified it. Then we tuned into the local radio to find out if anyone else had seen this UFO, but no one had reported it. Of course people do not want to be identified with anything extraterrestrial because they are often thought to be imagining things.

After I had made a telephone call to the late Graham Birdsall of *UFO Magazine* he suggested that I write my experience down as an article for the magazine. Also I drew a blank from local newspapers. Although silent, the craft may have been seen shooting away leaving a greyish vapour trail, unless we were meant to be the only witnesses.

Our next encounter can only be described as a living nightmare. On 3 October 1994, just before we (John and I) lost power to the engine of our car, the lights went out. On the A5 near to the New Inn, between Daventry, Buckby Wharf and Kilsby, travelling rather more slowly than the noisy heavy lorries, we had a very weird experience. I had noticed that there were lights in a field to my left and assuming them to be from a tractor working late into the night, to get some sort of task completed before the hired pieces of machinery were returned, I did not take a lot of notice. They were, I remember, directed downwards, as if to provide light as potatoes or something was being taken from the soil. There was no sign of workers and potato picking was usually finished by October, but I did not think it unusual. Tractors are used for so many tasks and to see lights at that time of night is not unusual.

"Silly b—!" I commented to my husband. "It is far too dark to see the potholes in the field. His tractor will turn over if he is not careful."

We were on our way home to Hillmorton after taking our son to Daventry to board a coach for Ireland for a holiday.

Then suddenly our car lights went out. Huge lorries continued to dash past, and I thought we might be hit from behind. Then the radio went dead. Then the engine stopped. Luckily we were near the kerb – we sat for a moment looking at one another, not daring to move or speak. The lorries hurtling past seemed to have strobe lights that lit up the interior of our little car. We were frightened. Would the lorries hit us? Could they see us in their headlights, which seemed to be so powerful?

"Good job I was driving," said John. "You would have been in the ditch by now."

I wondered later why I did not climb out of the car as my seat was near to the kerb. Was it because my husband could not? Was I afraid to leave the car and step into the traffic, or was I really too paralysed with fear to move? It did seem, for those few moments, unreal, as if I were watching someone else in the car. I have vivid flashbacks, whereas John can remember almost nothing except his incredulity that the engine had stopped.

Then suddenly, with no prompting whatsoever, the

radio came into life, startling us, and then the lights and then the engine started with no one touching any switches.

"John."

"Must have been a loose wire," he said, as usual being practical.

"Get me home." I was, for no reason, crying.

All the way home I wondered how a loose wire could have repaired itself. I thought it must have been several wires, as the radio, lights and engine must have independent wiring systems.

As we gathered our senses and moved off I thought it strange that the tractor had disappeared.

We arrived home safely but a little confused. The kitchen clock showed that the journey had taken much longer than usual. At least twenty minutes had been added to our journey from Daventry to Hillmorton. It had seemed a long time sitting in the car on the busy A5 and a frightening experience could play games with the time, but it did not seem many minutes at the time.

I still have nightmares, but on waking I remember only a little of the dreams. I only know for sure that the dreams are scary and that I wake in a hot sweat.

My husband never dreams, which I feel may be lucky; or if he does he remembers nothing of them. If I could find a hypnotist who would be willing to use a tape recorder and agree to give me the tape then I may consider regression. Why consider this? Because, like Elsie Oakensen, who was abducted from this area, I have also developed artistic skills, an interest in spiritual things (including crystals and dowsing) and archaeology.

In her book, Elsie Oakensen describes her abduction from outside a tiny village in Northamptonshire. On 22 November 1978 near the village of Stowe Nine Churches she was taken by extraterrestrials, but it was much later that she remembered the abduction after regression. However, she apparently suffered from the classic symptoms of abduction. Her artistic abilities began to emerge, she became psychic and her drawing skills included psychic art. Her book tells that her spiritual nature developed and she discovered healing powers and an interest in poetry writing.

Sometime after this revelation, another villager, Georgina Lawry, came forward to corroborate the sighting of a UFO spaceship at the same time on the same day as the one that Elsie witnessed.

Northamptonshire is a hot spot for sightings.

On the Warwickshire border with Northamptonshire there have been many sightings, and perhaps many are not recorded for fear of ridicule. From 1947 until 1996 I have, with others, witnessed many sightings. From nine years old to later in life I have seen triangles, saucers, cigars and lights in this area, stretching from the A5 and A428 out towards Coventry and beyond the Northamptonshire borders.

The late Graham Birdsall wrote in *UFO Magazine* that much abduction goes unpublished due to fear of ridicule by family and peers. That is the reason why until we retired in 2000 I dared not write of my own experiences.

When the American couple Betty and Barney Hill were abducted in September 1961 their story was ridiculed for many years; it is only now that all over the world their experiences are believed. Because they are from very different ethnic backgrounds they may have been of particular interest to the extraterrestrials.

Another abductee, Rachel Jones, whose experience was reported in *UFO Magazine*, thinks that there may be a government cover-up as her story tells of abductions at the ages of four, fourteen and twenty-four. No one apparently took her protestations seriously.

On 6 January 1995 BA pilots on a Boeing 747 flying from Milan over the Pennines back to Manchester Ringway Airport saw a UFO flying alongside their aeroplane. The crew was Captain Roger Wills and First Officer Mark Stuart. When the incident occurred they were flying at 13,000 feet. Both men witnessed that the UFO buzzed them.

In February 1958 Antonio Villas Boas, a twenty-three-year-old labourer living at São Francisco de Sales in Brazil was ploughing in the fields when he saw a UFO. He was allegedly taken and forced to have sex with a humanoid female who was only four feet tall. On his return home he had suffered radiation burns that could not be explained.

Budd Hopkins, a world expert on abductees, now believes that many more people will eventually come forward with their stories concerning what they believe to be real abductions, when loss of time cannot be explained.

Jacques Vallée submitted that maybe we live in a parallel dimension that can be accessed through time–space-continuum portals. This is in line with Einstein's space–time-continuum theory that light rays are bent because objects exert a gravitational pull that can bend light rays. This causes a warping of space – hence warp speed. Space doubles back on itself, creating a short cut that could enable faster-than-light travel. (Try folding a map into a tube and observe how this theory works.)

Heisenberg's uncertainty principle – that position and velocity cannot be measured at the same time (particle and compensatory) – appears to give some credence to this theory. As does the Schrödinger's-cat theory, where a thing can possibly be in two places at the same time. However, with parallel-universe theories the most unanswered question is usually what happens if time travellers go back in time and change something? The effect could be devastating for the present or the change may only happen in a parallel universe.

Jacques Vallée is reputed to believe that knowledge and insight flooded his mind after abduction, when he became a vegetarian, religious and an artist. He wondered if genetic engineering had taken place to facilitate this change in his behaviour.

In 1978 in Los Angeles, USA, Tracy Knapp was on a journey to Las Vegas with two friends when they were lifted out of their car, and later she discovered that she was pregnant. Could this have been an experiment by extraterrestrials? What happened to the child is not known.

In 1981 Karen Morgan had a mind scan and was stripped naked by her abductors, but she forgot the incident until it was revealed under hypnosis. She remembered the aliens abducting her again and removing a foetus to nurture as a hybrid. For what purpose they did not disclose. This could be the answer to what happened to Tracy Knapp.

In 1982 Barbara Archer was abducted for the third time. She remembered being taken before when she was only sixteen years old and at the age of twelve years. This is not unusual − several abductees have been taken several times over many years and have been too afraid to speak out.

In 1958 Jill Pinzarro was only nine years old when she was first taken and it happened again at eleven years old. This is an unusual case as she was taken up to the ship by means of some sort of elevator.

Biologist Dr Lyall Watson suggests in an article that during a dream we can bring forward suppressed reptilian memories that could possibly be sixty million years old. Distortion of memories during evolution could possibly account for this suppression. Carl Sagan and

Dr Watson agree that morphological similarities between dinosaurs and dragons have a hold on our imaginations. Aliens from our past or from the future, reptilian or Greys, eminent scientists and science-fiction writers agree on the characteristics of the visitors from space–time.

1. Height, six to eight feet – reptilians.
2. Height, three to four feet – Greys.
3. All reptilians or hybrids have some sort of scales.
4. Eyes, either black and large or wearing night-sight glasses.
5. Webbed feet, sometimes six fingers, sometimes only four fingers.
6. Have some way of communicating telepathically.
7. Do not wish the abductees permanent harm.
8. Implants are tracking devices.

Dr J. Alan Hyneck, who died in 1986, investigated physical trace cases according to the book *The World's Greatest UFO Stories*, page 483.

In 1985 Paul Bennevitz, a UFO researcher, suggested that his abduction and implants caused him to suffer a breakdown. He had seen vehicles powered by static electricity and also beam weapons when he was abducted. His friends hinted that a government misinformation campaign caused his breakdown in an attempt to cover up his experiences.

In 1981 Paul Villa, who lived in Apolinar, USA, died of cancer. He was of Native American and Spanish descent. Since he was five years old he had been in contact with aliens. He understood physics, engineering and mathematics and he served in the US Air Force. In 1953 a tall alien invited him to enter a spaceship, where aliens told him they had bases on the moon and on Phobos, a moon of Mars. US astronauts saw structures on the moon and recorded the sightings on a tape recorder. This tape is reported to still exist, as many have witnessed.

Bob Lazar, a physicist, is quoted in *UFO Magazine* as having seen flying saucers being back-engineered from captured alien craft in 1989. At Groom Lake facility in the USA many different species of aliens are living and working – whether by choice or force is not known. Bob Lazar's testimony was reviled, but now there is proof of his work as a physicist at the extraterrestrial facility. Naturally this work should be kept from the public so as not to cause a panic, and for reasons of national security, but there are times when the truth can be told.

Writer and UFO researcher Whitley Strieber witnessed the interview footage of an alien captured at Area 51, Groom Lake, USA, where it is thought the US Government employs extraterrestrials on top-secret technology projects. This allegedly shows a Grey with large black eyes set in a very large head on a small body. The US Government could authenticate the film, but they are unlikely to admit to its existence. Colonel Bob Dean, a UFO researcher, was convinced that the interview was real. He based this on the fact that the alien looks the same as other photographs he had seen of the bodies of aliens. Colonel Dean is reputed to believe that the CIA released the film either to test public opinion regarding the existence of aliens or to manipulate the public's attitude to their existence. (From Graham W. Birdsall.)

On 6 June 1884 in Dundy County, Southern Nebraska, the local press speculated that a craft from 'outer space' must have landed in their county. The investigators at the crash site discovered and recovered aluminium alloys that were unknown at that time.

At Aurora, Texas, on 19 April 1897 material gathered

from a UFO crash site was covered in hieroglyphic-like symbols. A body was found and it is alleged that the locals quickly buried it. The local authority denied all requests for an exhumation of the alien body.

On 13 September 1998 it was reported in local newspapers that dead aliens had been captured on film held by the KGB. One of the films was presumed to show a headless torso discovered in Western Siberia in March 1969.

In 1954 at Nellis Weapons Range, the Lockheed Aircraft Corporation developed a spy plane for the CIA comparable to the Stealth bomber.

As a child Bob Lazar had invented a motorbike that reached 350 miles an hour, and at the age of twenty-three he became a scientist who worked on secret programmes. He reputedly worked on the Strategic Defence Initiative called Star Wars at Los Alamos, New Mexico, USA. He also worked at Area 51, Groom Lake. In May 1989, on a television programme, he is alleged to have said, "Nine spaceships are housed at Area 51." The site S4 is next to Papoose Lake, and there were twenty-two engineers working there in November 1989. He said also that he saw a spaceship with chairs of some kind inside it that measured only one foot high. There were an anti-gravity field and a propulsion unit in the craft that he said he saw. The crews had large heads and were small Greys, the same as those seen in the autopsies. The extraterrestrials claimed to have come from Zeta Reticuli.

Bob Lazar added that in 1979 aliens had killed security staff at Area 51 and it was allegedly hushed up for security reasons. Continuing, he maintained that technological proof could be found at this facility. He also disclosed that in 1995, in Germany, canisters containing dead aliens were found. He went on to suggest that the USA spend 35 billion dollars on research each year.

Physicist Stanton Friedman discredited Lazar. However, researcher George Knapp discovered Lazar's name in an internal telephone directory and a salary statement issued to Lazar by the US Department of Naval Intelligence – proof that Lazar told the truth all along. (From *UFO Magazine*.)

The incident at Varginha, Brazil, mentioned earlier, took place on 20 January 1996 in a park in the northern suburb of Jardin Andere. Five firemen saw a small biped with blood-red eyes in the gardens. It ran and hid among the shrubs, and the terrified firemen called out the troops to investigate. General Sergio Goelho Lima sent out his troops immediately. A local resident, Henrique Jose, watched the alien being put into a secure crate and it was taken away by the General's troops. Three girls (housemaids) told the investigator Ubirijara Rodrigues that they also saw the strange creature. They were Liliane Fatima Silva, aged sixteen years; Valquira, her sister, aged fourteen years; and Katia Andrada Xavier, aged twenty-two years. There were over sixty sightings of a similar creature in Rio de Janeiro, 300 miles from Varginha, but it was recorded that the two aliens were captured at Varginha. The bodies were taken, it is alleged, to a military school at Tres Coracoes, where two days later, on 22 January, a policeman died because he had been bitten by one of the two aliens. The authorities gave no satisfactory explanation to his family.

One of the aliens was taken to Varginha Regional Hospital and then transferred to Varginha Humanitas Hospital, two miles away. It was reported that the creature died on Monday 22 January 1996, two days after its capture. It is alleged that fifteen doctors, army staff and police witnessed the creature in the hospital. The extraterrestrial had only three fingers, no sex organs and jointed legs and seemed to be of a reptilian nature. The body was taken to the University of Campinas, 200 miles away. What happened to it after its examination is not clear.

The Brazilian Air Force tracked a UFO in the same area. However, its trajectory did not prove if it landed or crashed. Speculation was rife. Could there have been a third alien? On 21 April 1997 at 9 p.m. at the zoo in Varginha an extraterrestrial was seen by a prominent member of the zoo staff, who was very shaken by the encounter.

The editor of Brazil's UFO magazine, A. J. Gevaerd, is quoted as saying that there is nothing to prohibit ufological research and "There may soon be a global change of consciousness regarding the subject of UFOs."

CHAPTER EIGHT

ALIEN TECHNOLOGY

It has been suggested that alien technology is far in advance of our own. SETI is transmitting messages to show the location of our solar system in the galaxy, beaming them out to the further reaches of the galaxy. DNA and the atomic numbers of hydrogen, oxygen, carbon, nitrogen and phosphorus are being sent beyond the boundaries of our solar system. An American astronomer, F. Drake, has estimated that at least forty planets in our galaxy have technology similar to our own. Humans have only travelled approximately half a million miles to the moon; he estimates that to reach us the extraterrestrials would have to travel at least a billion miles. He has reached the conclusion that their power source would be beyond human imagination. Water in liquid form is so precious, but beyond the Earth only a small fraction of planets may be capable of containing it. Mars does not have enough mass to keep water on its surface, although there may be ice on the poles. Venus and Mercury are so hot that water would boil on their surfaces. The gas giants and the rocky planets are also not suitable as they cannot sustain an atmosphere. If aliens come to take our water, then a drought so terrible will occur that the Earth may never recover. Is it possible that extraterrestrials have a hand in global warming?

Humans may become slaves to the invaders as all

civilisations in the past (and even some today) have exploited slavery. Only the fittest men and females of breeding age will be kept alive to increase the stock, as farmers do with domestic cattle, etc. Aliens would not waste valuable resources on the weak. A great thinker, Zachariah Sitchen, believes that the human race is a genetically altered species and that the implants found in abductees are extraterrestrial in origin due to their isotopic ratios. Implants were examined at 1,000-times magnification using an electron microscope and they were found to contain a 'fish hook' with a T-bar. One rod had a carbon core and the other rod an iron core. The carbon rod was electrically conductive while the iron rod was magnetic. There was attraction between the two, and silicate crystals encircled both rods. These combinations were used in a crystal set – quartz and copper were used in a similar way to receive signals on the primitive wireless set. It has been scientifically proved that the isotopic ratios from these implants were not of earthly origin. It has been suggested, in many quarters, that the implants found on the abductees could be tracking devices to follow the progress of the implanted individual.

In September 1950 a device was tested that apparently contravenes Newton's third law of action–reaction. Thomas Black demonstrated this device, called electrogravitics, for the US navy. The demonstration of electrogravitics was secret and called Deep Black. *Jane's Defence Weekly* asked, 'Could mach 3 have been achieved in the 1950's via electrogravitics?'

Great rocks may have been levitated and moved by the knowledge of electrogravitics, historians suggest, to explain the lifting of great stones and their alignment with such regularity.

A news item appeared in *The Engineer* magazine on 31 March 2000: 'The military wing of BA systems has confirmed that it has launched an anti-gravity research programme called Project Greenglow.' However, free energy is not in the interest of many powerful institutions. The technology to power vehicles from water has, it is alleged, existed since as far back as 1980.

An article in *UFO Magazine* in September 2003 reported that a levitation machine was being developed by NASA. According to the article this seeming miracle could be achieved by passing 20,000 volts through strips of tin foil on an arrangement of equilateral triangles.

In various texts it has been suggested that former NATO general and US Secretary of State Alexander Haig and General Vernon Walters under DCI George Bush, US Ambassador during the Reagan era, may have been aware of these projects. Also the head of the military arm of the Vatican, the Grand Knight of the Sovereign Military Order of Malta, may have been made aware of these experiments.

Thomas Townsend Brown from Ohio is alleged to have seen capacitors (electronic components that can store and release a charge). Capacitors would facilitate a UFO to travel with no fuel on board and there would be no moving parts to take up valuable space.

We do not notice air until we have none. We ignore the wind until it blows. Fish in a tank won't notice the water until the tank is empty. There are many scientists who agree that zero-point energy exists. Physicists explain the effects as electricity, magnetism and heat.

Writing in the science journal *Nature*, the astronomer Joan Einastox, at Tartu observatory in Estonia, discovered that the distribution of the universe resembles a three-dimensional chessboard and that the galaxy clusters are arranged in a kind of lattice. This also suggests parallel universes.

Data from the Hubble Space Telescope in 1995 suggested that if life were to be found it would be on 16 Cygni C and 47 Ursae Majoris B as their moons have the components to support life. These findings are from Darren Williams and colleagues at Pennsylvania State University. Where magnetic fields and temperatures are right then plants and animals can flourish. These two planets are exactly in the same position in relation to their stars as the Earth is to our sun. Their moons have oceans, masses at least one-tenth the size of Earth and have maintained an atmosphere for millions of years. *Nature* magazine suggested that Europa and Io could possibly sustain a form of life if the photographs from Voyager can be believed.

Father Jose Funes, who has been in charge of the Vatican's observatory for two years, was quoted in the *Daily Express* on Thursday 15 May 2008: 'The Pope accepts there is life on other planets and believes it is all part of God's plan.' Pope Benedict XVI has let it be known there is no conflict between believing in God and in the possibility of 'extraterrestrial brothers', perhaps more evolved than humans. There is a branch of astronomy, astro-biology, which looks specifically at this question and has made significant advances in recent years.

On 2 July 1947 there was a terrific thunderstorm over Roswell army airfield in New Mexico. At the time this airfield was the only home of an atomic bomber squad in the world – 509 Bomb Group. William Ware 'Mac' Brazel, foreman of a sheep ranch belonging to J. Foster, thirty miles from the cattle town of Corona, saw strange lights and on investigation found shiny material that resumed its shape when bent.

On 8 July the story of his find ran in the local newspaper. The wireless publicised the incident and a UFO incident was broadcast to locals. Then the army was contacted. Baffling counter-stories emerged. Locals thought that alien bodies were taken to Walter Reed Hospital. Secret files alleged that the Washington Hospital performed autopsies on the dead bodies of aliens and even kept one or more alive. Nursing staff reported that bodies only four feet high with only four fingers and large heads were operated on.

Colonel Philip Corso was an intelligence officer on General Douglas MacArthur's staff in Korea and served for four years on President Dwight Eisenhower's security staff. He was based at Fort Riley in Kansas in July 1947. Colonel Corso allegedly saw sealed boxes containing thick liquid in which submerged four-foot humanoids with four fingers, grey snaky skin and large heads were suspended.

Mac Brazel testified to reporters that only five hours after the incident the government denied his testament, as did the 8th Army Air Force at Fort Worth.

This incident was given little publicity until 1978, when by chance an investigator into UFO activity was given several clues concerning the Roswell incident. It is now widely believed that we have benefited from this crash by processing information found at the crash site at Groom Lake, Area 51, Nevada. Optic fibres, night vision, lasers, particle beams and integrated circuits may have been advanced from back-engineering information gathered at UFO crash sites.

According to *UFO Magazine*, a statement made in the House of Lords by Lord Strabolgi stated that the Horseguards were given a stern warning not to tell anyone, not even wives, what he or she knew to be the truth concerning extraterrestrial activity.

If, as we suspect, UFO propulsion systems harness magnetic forces, and they can generate antigravitons that nullify gravitational forces, then they need little or no energy to power their machines. Could this be the key to propellant-less propulsion? If so it must remain a secret because of the devastating effect on the world's economy. Microwave radiation may be the cause of engine cut-out, which has happened in so many cases when travelling along certain routes by car. My husband and I have experienced this on the A5 near Daventry, Northamptonshire. If the extraterrestrial craft can create an atmosphere to surround their craft, that is in effect an anti-gravity field. As there is no discernible sonic boom when they shoot away at incredible speeds this could be because the force field keeps air flowing around their craft at subsonic speed.

In 1960 in Colorado, USA, a rim around a craft was seen to close, probably to cause less friction as it journeyed to its destination.

It may be possible that manipulation of gravity can cause space–time warps, where the very fabric of time and space allows the craft to travel along the contours of time and space without incurring inertia.

It was reported in *UFO Magazine* in October 1988 that the US Government may have, or may know about, a secret group connected with extraterrestrial activity, called Aviary. It was also alleged, according to Bruce Maccabee, an optical physicist who had served in the US Navy Surface Weapons Laboratory, that this organisation does exist. What is intriguing is whether MJ12 controls Aviary or does Aviary control MJ12? There seems to be no congressional scrutiny on these activities and no official budgets – therefore officially Aviary does not exist. Could the whole issue be misinformation to hide the real organisation, a hoax to throw the gullible off the scent or something even more sinister? We can only guess and make up our own minds on these important issues that could ultimately affect us all on this Earth.

Quote from the late G. W. Birdsall: 'People must know the truth.'

Beagle 2 was launched from Baikonar spaceport, Kazakhstan, and voyaged to Mars to seek out signs of life. The European Space Agency (ESA) vehicle landed on Christmas Day. The inconclusive findings did indicate the existence of ice, but generally the findings will not be public knowledge for many years to come, if ever. Panic would ensue if it were admitted that alien life does exist in this part of the galaxy.

When Dr Gilbert Levin, former NASA mission scientist

responsible for detecting experiments on the NASA Viking mission in 1976, detected life and had evidence to prove that it existed, it is believed that his other experiments were rejected by the ESA and NASA. He discovered strange signs of life, including microbes giving off gas where no organic matter was thought to exist.

Dr Tom van Flandern, a scientist, has staked his reputation on there being life on Mars. Mars changes; photographs differ at different times of the year, seeming to prove that there are seasons on the surface of the planet. Could there possibly be envious eyes waiting to harvest our vast oceans? Water is a scarce commodity in the universe and it is a rich resource, meaning that we on Earth could be envied by watchers from afar. Whoever, or whatever, may be watching would have to settle their people here on our planet to discover how to transport the water and whether to desalinate it. However, first they would have to either conquer the Earth or come to an agreement. Options would be to annihilate the population or subdue them into slavery or assimilate and cause hybridisation of the whole planet. Could this already be under way and the cause of all the abductions and also the cattle mutilations? People of the Earth would have to be studied before colonisation could be implemented, and the cattle appear to accept their fate without a struggle. This of course would appeal to any enemy, as it is easier to subdue a passive population than to fight a violent one. This would take time, and if time is running out for their home world then more abduction should be expected. Maybe if the abductees were taken seriously, then governments all over the world could give more help and guidance to them. There are too many cases of abductions for them all to be imagination. Alien technology may already be in the possession of governments as computerisation is evolving at a terrifying rate of knots.

There exists a speed at least 100 times faster than the speed of light! This remarkable statement comes from Mitch Battros (ECTV). He says, 'New scientific studies show that there is in fact a speed faster than light.'

Some recent scientific research suggests 1,000 times faster, including research by Dr Tom van Flandern, who worked for twenty years at NASA and at the naval observatory, where he became chief of the Celestial Mechanics Branch.

Meta research in 1991 at Washington revealed, 'It is possible that there has been, and currently is, extraterrestrial travel.' (Go to www.interseti.com.)

Experiments on 8 September 2002, when Jupiter passed in front of radio quasar JO 843+1835, showed that gravity travels at 1,106 times the speed of light. This suggests more work is needed on the anti-gravity experiments, as it is alleged the propulsion of flying saucers is based on anti-gravity.

The superstring theory, believed by many scientists, is that at least ten dimensions with six rolled up on the subsonic level could and do exist. This is beyond the comprehension of the normal human being. Could Einstein's theory be reformulated to make gravity analogous to electromagnetic radiation, and in so doing allow the speed of gravity to be determined?

Where is zero point? Should scientists be investigating areas like this with more speed before it is too late to stop any invasion by an as yet unknown route?

It is widely accepted that the mineral quartz produces an electrical field when pressure is applied to it, and the information is stored. If the information is to be released at a later time, then what triggers the release?

The answers to so many questions may be within the reach of humankind if we know where to look, and if alien technology is available then it should be embraced.

It is generally acknowledged that the universe may have natural wormholes, although these have yet to be discovered. Professor Sergei Krasnikov of the Pulkovo Observatory in St Petersburg suggested in the *New Scientist* magazine that it might be possible to create artificial wormholes. Einstein, in his theory of relativity, hinted at the existence of wormholes throughout the galaxy. However, large amounts of matter would have to be compressed to form the immense gravitational fields needed to warp space and time. The reflection that would be seen by looking into a wormhole would be the other end. After construction the two ends of the wormhole would be near each other, but to travel by wormhole one end would be left in the laboratory and the other end would have to be transported to its destination by spaceship. Then, and only then, the two points, even if millions of miles apart, would be connected by instant travel links. But the big problem is knowing where the other end would lead – we can only find out by travelling through the wormhole itself. Professor Krasnikov, writing in the *New Scientist*, predicts that a wormhole could one day connect Vega and the Earth.

Every 5,000 years the Earth experiences a solar-inspired catastrophe, where mountains become seabeds and the seabeds become mountains. Noah's flood may have been one of these as it is documented all over the known world in libraries and art. As the sunspot cycle is 96 micro-cycles of magnetic activity, common sense tells us that the effect upon our Earth must be tremendous. After the ice ages and the many floods, how could so many treasures suddenly appear from a world where only ice existed?

In his book *Chariots of the Gods* Erich Von Daniken writes of flying serpents and a culture older than the usual evolutionary theory that 12,000 years ago civilisations and cultures capable of making treasures did not exist –

well, not on the Earth. He also says that in Iraq there has been found a cut-crystal lens alleged to belong to a culture far older than was imagined before. Dr Wilhelm Konig, writing about Baghdad, Iraq, said that electrical batteries have been found that have been dated as being 2,000 years old. The composition of the batteries: 'solder Cu 60/40 Pb, tin alloys also present'. The batteries were sealed with asphalt and bitumen. There were also iron rods and copper cylinders corroded by acid.

Twentieth-century scientists have, it is believed, caught sound between two reflecting mirrors and caused the sound to levitate small pieces of stone. Stone discs that resonate were found with the tiny skeletons in Koffiefontein and also in Ireland. Some scientists and science writers have suggested that sound waves could have been used to levitate the perfectly aligned stones in some ancient Mexican walls. The Holy Bible tells us that the walls of Jericho came tumbling down when the trumpets blew. Someone was given the knowledge that sound waves had great power when co-ordinated and calibrated.

The ancient Egyptians knew about the laws of sound frequency and the diatonic ratio between music and maths, the curator at the Cairo Museum told us when we visited several years ago. He explained that sand in a box would form into one large circle when a certain frequency of sound was transmitted and several smaller circles would appear at another frequency. He also demonstrated the same technique using water. Unfortunately I did not have a notebook with me.

It is alleged that an aluminium belt has been dated to a culture much older than many experts believed possible. Also in Delhi there is to this day a non-rusting iron pillar. How is this possible when the date suggests that there were no living humans at that time?

In Cambodia, information concerning the ancient temples has revealed a few surprises: the carvings appear to relate to a time in Angkor when the temples were built by angels, and by small genies and giant people called the Solaman.

In the Sahara Desert there are petroglyphs standing nineteen feet high and the carvings tell that spacemen in suits came from the sky gods 6,000 years ago and painted these stones. (From *Circles and Standing Stones,* by Evan Hadingham, published by Heinemann.)

Robert Temple's book *The Sirius Mystery* tells us that the Dogon tribes in Africa know about the double star in Sirius that cannot be seen from the Earth. They also have a petroglyph that is purported to show a map of the Milky Way.

The Mayan culture told stories that reveal they were visited by ancient astronauts with advanced technology.

In Guatemala there is a stela that depicts a reptilian with a chain as a tail. Could this be a pet or a servant?

We must assume that extraterrestrials have visited Earth, and maybe they still do. The evidence is pointing to something extraordinary that is happening, and not all the evidence is available to the general public because of national security and to avoid a panic.

On 7 November 1975 at the Malmstrom airbase at Lewistown, Montana, USA, launch targets were altered after a UFO flew over the base. In all, twenty-four UFOs were sighted that day. (Michael Heseman.)

An interview with astronomer Walter Webb at the Pease airbase, USA, revealed that the US had tracked several UFOs over the White Mountains in 1961.

When astronomer Marjorie Fish gave an interview she revealed that the star map drawn by both Betty and Barney Hills was an exact match of Zeta Reticuli, fifty light years away from the Earth. Could it be that they were taken as examples of different cultures, as Barney is Ethiopian and Betty a white American?

Senator Barry Goldwater was, it is alleged, denied access to secret documents concerning UFO research at the Wright Patterson airbase in 1970. There are thought to be aliens helping with back-engineering. Night sights, advanced computers and even human alien clones have been suggested as part of the clandestine experiments.

Robert Kilroy Silk in 1979 asked a question in the Houses of Parliament: Could he have an explanation as to why the US Air Force had chased a UFO between Southport and Blackpool, England? "If there is a cover-up it is of immense proportions."

CHAPTER NINE

THE LATE GRAHAM W. BIRDSALL

It was on 14 August 2006 that a television programme caught my attention. I could hardly believe what I was hearing and seeing. "Original footage of the moon landing has been lost!" Surely this must be a joke! No, the broadcaster was serious – not just one can of film, but several cans. Suddenly I remembered an article that I had read somewhere! This, I seemed to recall, was an incident from several years ago.

I searched through my copies of *UFO Magazine* and found the film dated from 1947: 'Birdsall Confirms Date of Alien Autopsy Film.' Kodak's Copenhagen office had, it seemed, confirmed the authenticity of a film on the alien autopsy that had taken place after the Roswell flying-saucer crash in the USA. The end markings on the film clearly showed that the film was manufactured in 1947. This did not in any way prove that the films were taken at that time – only the date of manufacture of the film. However, it was of a type that would have deteriorated fairly quickly if it had not been used in a short time frame. The loss of the moon-landing film reminded me of the controversy over the 1947 film.

Nellis Air Force Base, Nevada was to become known as Area 51, the secret base where it was believed the parts of the crashed spaceship were kept in 1947 before being taken to a secret location. It was on 31 May 1947 that a farmer called Brazel saw and handled pieces of a UFO from the crash site. The US Government took this to Nellis airbase for testing. Brazel was ordered to give up all the debris that he had collected from the farm where he worked, and later the government informed him that, although it was only a weather balloon that had crashed, he must also give back the samples he had given to his young son. (His son travelled to England to give lectures in 2008.)

Graham Birdsall was determined to get at the truth. It is alleged, in *The World's Greatest Atlas*, that he contacted Kodak's Copenhagen office to ask about the film's edge markings. A square plus a triangle meant 1947 manufacture. They confirmed the authenticity of the alien-autopsy film. Peter Milson, a senior manager at Kodak in England, did not know of Bufora's press claim that Kodak had previously tested the film. Salesmen at Kodak agreed that the film logs confirmed 1947 was the date of manufacture of the film itself, but not of the processing of the film. Is it possible that Santilli obtained an old film and then used it at a much later date? Not possible. This type of film must be used before the deterioration date.

The alien-autopsy footage that was shown on television in August 1995 was not given to Kodak. The frames of this film were not tested, although several requests were made. Tony Amato, a Kodak specialist, insisted, it is alleged, that he did not ever receive the film to authenticate. However, someone at Copenhagen did authenticate the film, and the marking details matched up with the date 1947.

Bob Shell, a US legal consultant on photography at the FBI, made a chemical analysis of the film. He, it is alleged, considered that this confirmed manufacture before 1956. Because of the unstable nature of the film, it could be genuine, as this type of film must be processed within two years of manufacture. It was a 16-mm Safety Super XX Panchromatic film.

Bufora's Philip Mantle, a military man, said that the

alien in the autopsy film is identical to the ones he saw with his own eyes in 1947.

Investigators Wrigglesworth and Spoor, who lived near to Lowestoft in 1997, were one of many partnership UFO investigators in Britain. Graham W. Birdsall offered to authenticate a piece of their film footage when they met at the UFO conference in Laughlin, Nevada. (David Dane, Norfolk ufologist.)

Many people who have seen the footage believe that it shows a craft of extraterrestrial origin. However, George Wingfield urged scepticism, although even he had to admit that something strange was going on in the skies over Norfolk.

In 1951, when a huge mother ship was seen over the Norfolk town of Gorleston-on-Sea near to Great Yarmouth, I was only thirteen years old and staying with an aunt and uncle in their small café in Bulls' Lane near to the quay. There were many adult and child witnesses, although we children were told not to 'make things up' and military advice was we should not discuss it at all. This was very frustrating for an enquiring mind with lots of imagination. To disagree with your elders in those days meant a good thrashing. I was lucky staying with understanding relatives; at home it would have been another matter. Some of my friends were punished for talking nonsense, and as the years passed they would of course keep quiet for fear of further ridicule. However, to our surprise, the fishermen were all too eager to talk about the spaceship, as they called it.

Some of the herring fishers were from Scotland and had spent most of their lives at sea, where, they told us children, they had seen many strange lights and objects on clear nights. Only in calm weather did they see spaceships. They described some as round and some as triangular. Always they were silent.

In 1998 Spoor, the investigator, reported seeing shining orbs over the sea. (From *The World's Greatest Atlas*.)

While many fakes have been proved, some reports will always remain an enigma. This was proved when President Truman's file on the Majestic 12 Commission to investigate UFOs was investigated. Grunge / Blue Book's Special Report 13 found that a certain number of sightings were genuine.

Petty Officer Milton of the US Navy, when he was quartermaster under the commander-in-chief of the Pacific Fleet, is reputed to have seen an actual photograph of Greys. A statement was allegedly issued that the Greys were communicating from a dying planet orbiting Betelgeuse. (From *The World's Greatest Atlas*.) It was also stated that, in return for alien technology secrets, aliens were being allowed to take humans and animals away for experiments in cloning and for hybridisation. Mutilation of cattle and human abductions may be proof of this interaction between known extraterrestrials and humans.

Graham W. Birdsall will be forever in our collective memory as the bravest exponent of UFO sightings. His publications showed no fear of ridicule, and I believe that he was sincere in all his editorial work in the many issues of *UFO Magazine*. He died on 11 September 2003. RIP.

CHAPTER TEN

MODERN TIMES

Under the USA's Freedom of Information Acts, it was May 2003 when this information was released into the public domain. According to newspapers at the time, when Neil Armstrong set foot on the moon, the *Apollo 11* astronaut said, "I probably made fifty significant observations in this period." He was alluding, it is alleged, to UFO sightings.

The debriefing texts and NASA mission reports relating to Buzz Aldrin and Michael Collins are still classified. But some expressions allegedly used by the astronauts suggest that UFOs were seen:

ALDRIN: "Day one, unusual things seen."
ALDRIN: "Could it be the S-1VB?"
ALDRIN: ". . . very sizeable dimension, a cylinder . . ."
COLLINS: ". . . out of the window an' there it was".
ARMSTRONG: ". . . like an open suitcase".
ARMSTRONG: ". . . or really two rings . . . connected".

(From *UFO Magazine*, May 2003, and from a book by Robert Godwin published by Apogee Books, Canada.)

In 1989 Colonel John Blaha, in Houston, Texas, informed NASA of UFO activity surrounding his spaceship and allegedly said, "This is *Discovery*. We still have the alien spacecraft under observation."

In 1997 the Mir space station was hit by something and the force of the impact was enough to damage the station. (From *UFO Magazine*, June 1997.)

In June 1965 James McDivitt and Ed White, astronauts aboard the *Gemini* spacecraft over Hawaii, saw something and took evasive action. A D-notice has been put on their photographs and information relating to this incident is restricted.

When Edwin Buzz Aldrin and Neil Armstrong landed on the moon on 21 July 1969 they allegedly reported on tape, "These babies are huge, sir – enormous. Oh, my God, you would not believe it: I am telling you there are other spacecraft out there, lined up on the far side of the crater rim and they are on the moon watching us." He continued: "I can't go into details except to say that their ships are bigger and far superior to ours."

There are no incriminating photographs in the public domain at the moment. Everything seems to have been hidden.

In 1951 it was reported that Donald Slayton and fellow astronauts flying a P-51 fighter aircraft saw what they believed to be a UFO. It was only three feet in diameter.

James Lovell and Frank Borman, flying in the *Gemini* spacecraft in December 1965, saw a UFO during their fourteen-day mission.

There is a suggestion that those responsible for the photographs of the moon landings may have added telltale signs to enable future scientists to decode these pictures. This suggests that evidence could have been hidden of past civilisations on the moon or of evidence seen by the astronauts. (From Mr David Percy, a photographer writing in the *Fortean Times* magazine.)

On 5 February 1971 Edgar Mitchell on the *Apollo 14* mission was witness to something unusual. In 1973 he formed the Institute of Noetic Sciences to research spiritual energy and psychic abilities. It is alleged that he believes extraterrestrial beings have been on Earth for many decades.

On 30 July 1971 the *Apollo 15* mission affected James Irwin so much that he turned to God on returning to Earth.

On 21 April 1972, after the *Apollo 16* mission Charles Duke also became very religious.

On 11 December 1972 Harrison Schmitt is reputed to have found Helium 3 on the moon – a new source of energy. This was not widely reported.

In 1973 on Skylab 2 Alan Bean, Jack Lousman and Owen Garrot, approximately 300 miles above the Earth, watched a UFO for ten minutes. When approached for confirmation, apparently NASA would not confirm or deny this incident.

In 1979 Maurice Chatelain worked for NASA. He claimed that a cover-up was ordered to hide the *Apollo 11* photographs. These were the ones taken by Buzz Aldrin in 1969, when he and Neil Armstrong landed on the moon on 21 July. They allegedly showed something that was seen by the two astronauts, described as being enormous and watching them from the rim of a moon crater. A newspaper in Moscow printed an article by Dr Vladimir Azhazda, a physicist, suggesting that NASA did censor the photographs for reasons of national security.

It is alleged that, under the seabed of the Gulf of Mexico, 2,800 feet below the sea floor, in 1997, the contractors Parsons discovered a vast complex of passageways. The construction engineer who reported this told reporters, "The construction presupposes the presence of live human beings living in places that were installed in the Atlantic Ocean basin."

This also suggests that extraterrestrial beings may only survive in a controlled atmosphere created especially for their existence. This may not be possible on terra firma, where the atmosphere cannot be as well regulated.

The Sycamore facility near San Diego, USA, is reputed to have housed aliens of some kind. The well-concealed entrance was through a normal semi-detached house. (This ploy was also used to conceal the entrance to a bolt-hole that was prepared for Sir Winston Churchill during the war years.) Boring machines were used to cut through the 2,000-feet-thick chalk stratum.

In the North Sea there may be subterranean tunnels and sea bases as unconventional flying objects have been seen diving into and out of the sea at various times by reliable witnesses.

Cheyenne Mountain in the USA has a maglev shuttle running at incredible speeds right up to the Pentagon, it is alleged. The maglev can travel at 2,000 miles an hour to transport important people away from the capital when the need arises.

In New Mexico there are said to be clandestine tunnels that could be connected to the White Sands Missile Range.

NSA headquarters at Fort Meade, Maryland, Washington and Baltimore may also have a complicated subterranean complex. This could be used to eavesdrop on the whole world if the need arises. Reliable unnamed witnesses tell of twenty floors completed in 1970. The work, they allege, continued in secret.

At China Lake, California, in 1964, the US Army Corps kept weapons 4,000 feet below the surface. (From Richard Saunders.)

Humans are abducted by extraterrestrials so that they can be trained to mentally communicate with the aliens, it has been suggested. Where these go-betweens are housed is not clear, but the suggestion is that the China Lake facility would be ideally suited to this clandestine programme. (From Dan Sherman, US Air Force.)

A contributor to the magazine *Nexus* maintains that a living machine, with organic and inorganic components, exists at Area 51. (From *Nexus*, 1971.)

It is well known that in the Yucca Mountains in Nevada, USA, there is a nuclear storage facility deep below the ground.

It has been reported that in Norway there are subterranean tunnels containing secret weapons of unknown origin.

According to Richard Saunders, writing in *UFO Magazine*, 'Credible rumours recur that the Canadians have manufactured a saucer design that has been under development for at least two years in the 1950s.' The saucer was said to have been manufactured by the Canadian Aircraft Company.

Einstein believed that two worlds could co-exist in different dimensions, each invisible to the other.

Scientists are not easily fooled and when Paul Santorini stated that he believed extraterrestrials did visit Earth, the Greek Astronomical Society at a conference in February 1967 would not believe him. Santorini expressed a view that plants, animals and humans were taken for experimentation, but without evidence his words fell on deaf ears.

In Illinois, USA, the Centre for UFO Studies, founded

by Dr J. Allen Hynek, is reputed to have photographic evidence of millions of sightings of extraterrestrial craft.

Until governments can be certain that UFOs are not antagonistic it is considered, by most, that the wisest course of action is to keep the public in ignorance to avoid worldwide panic. Remember *The War of the Worlds*?

On 11 September 2001 President George Bush witnessed the crash site outside Shanksville, Pennsylvania, where forty innocents and four hijackers were killed when a United Airlines Boeing 757-200 crashed. Only one piece of human spine survived the 'accident'. This eight-inch piece of human bone was all that could be identified. The rest of the passengers of Flight UA93 were reduced to charcoal. Three F16s patrolled the sky over the White House, Washington DC.

Bill Wright, piloting a single-engined Piper aeroplane, had been suddenly told to turn and land immediately, without explanation, by the control tower. He could see Flight UA93 three miles away.

The FBI has allegedly gagged a call made by Edward Felt, a passenger on that flight, using his mobile just before the crash. Interesting!

When questioned about UFO activity, Dr David Clarke of Sheffield University said the mystery "may never be resolved".

The Vatican theologian Monsignor Corrado Balducci has been quoted as saying, "Extraterrestrial contact is a real phenomenon and the Vatican has set up a commission to enlighten the public to an indoctrination policy."

The Holy Bible tells us God made man in his own image.

In 1942 in Newbiggin-by-the-Sea, England, Albert Lancashire, a private in the army, floated up towards a light source. It was not reported what happened next. At the time of the incident this was not thought to be of any significance and it was explained as being due mainly to the compounds in the air in wartime. It was recorded, however, as being unusual.

In 1947 in Washington, USA, Fred Johnson, a prospector in the Cascade Mountains, witnessed six discs in the sky.

On 28 July 1994 a US Air Force pilot called his control tower, Mexico 180: "UFO seen – what instructions?"
"Maintain heading and altitude," he was told.

In July 1994 Captain R. Cervantes Ruano had a mid-air collision with an unseen UFO. Flight 129 radioed to the control tower that the 109 passengers and crew had seen two UFOs. The control tower admitted that at least two near misses from UFOs occur each week in their area.
One has to ask why governments hide or do not admit to the evidence.

The US Air Force gave, it is alleged, secret orders on how to deal with UFOs. Would this have been done if the government dismissed out of hand the existence of extraterrestrials? The orders stated that if a UFO was within the pilot's sight he must capture it at all costs. Unfortunately on 7 January 1948 Captain Thomas Mantell Junior took these instructions literally and died when his P51 Mustang fighter plane climbed above the recommended height of 14,000 feet. He subsequently crashed to his death.
At Godman airbase, Fort Knox, Kentucky, many people had witnessed seeing a UFO hovering above them in a cloudless sky. This was at 1.15 p.m. The chief of police called Godman airbase and suggested that they call Wright Patterson airbase.
At about 1.35 that same afternoon the radar operators at the base saw a blip at around 13,000 feet. The ground

staff could see the UFO hovering and they witnessed this for half an hour. They estimated its size as being 200 feet across. At this time the leader of four P51 Mustang fighter planes, Captain Thomas Mantell Junior, radioed that they were ten miles south of Godman. His instructions were to track the UFO. However, one of the fighters was very low on fuel and had to land back at base while the other three continued to track the UFO. Without oxygen, two of the other pilots thought it wise to return when they were at 22,000 feet. The recommended height without oxygen is 14,000 feet for that type of aircraft. Naturally they tried to follow the secret instructions to the letter, but at that height without oxygen it was not safe to continue.

Captain Mantell continued the chase. He reported that the UFO was approximately 200 feet across and travelling at a speed of 200 knots. The size was the same as the control tower had estimated. What happened next no one knows for sure. In a field near Franklin, Kentucky, the body of Captain Mantell and the wreck of his plane were found. His watch had stopped at 3.18 p.m. and it was 1.15 when the UFO was first spotted – two hours later the Captain died in the crash. Could he have been under orders not to give up the chase and to capture at all costs? Whatever the orders, he paid the supreme penalty for carrying them out.

On 23 November 1957 in Levelland, Texas, USA, nine car engines simultaneously stopped working for no apparent reason. Something or someone had interfered with the electrics on all nine cars. It is amazing that no accidents were recorded.

In 1960 in the Mojave Desert, William Shatner saw a UFO when he had lost contact with his friends. It is alleged that he followed the UFO and it led him back to his friends.

The broadcaster Jonathan Ross saw a UFO when he was a schoolboy.

In Scotland there is a plaque to commemorate an incident in 1979 when Bob Taylor saw small men that attacked him and ripped his clothing, even splitting his trousers. They reputedly came from an alien spacecraft, which left tracks ten feet long and seven feet wide.

In 1969 in Alaska bright glowing objects were seen measuring seventy feet in diameter. They emerged from the water and then shot into the sky at roughly 7,000 miles an hour. These craft were tracked on radar. This incident was reported by a secret agent at 'crypto level fourteen extra-sensitive material handling security clearance'. He of course could not be named, as this is normal procedure. He admitted to working in the code room at a naval communications station in San Francisco, USA, in 1969. The message was 'priority' from a ship near to Alaska and classified as 'top secret'. According to *UFO Magazine*, he was later revealed to be Dan Willis, a US Navy officer.

More than 4,000 cases of encounters that have left a physical trace behind have been recorded. These are classified as CE2.

The most important encounter ever recorded occurred to sixteen-year-old Ron Johnson on 2 November 1971. What he saw was an eight-foot-diameter extraterrestrial craft. He approached this and stood too near. The consequence was that he became blind soon after the encounter. His parents had seen the lights of the craft glowing; they also witnessed to seeing the glowing circle of light emanating from the soil where the spaceship had landed. They both smelt something like sulphur. It may have been residue from an engine containing cobalt as this gives a sulphur smell, as witnessed in the deep mines where small skeletons and discs were found. This smell gave rise to the theory that maybe the Devil has something to do with the extraterrestrials. The sheriff at the time was Ralph Enlow, who took the soil samples to be expertly examined. The white powder residue turned to brown while being examined.

After five years, in 1976, the ring on the soil where the craft landed was still visible to the naked eye. This report came from the eminent Dr J. Hynek, who saw the evidence himself in 1976 and wrote a report for *UFO Magazine*.

Around 200,000 adults go missing each year and there is no official register of names and addresses.

Former radar operator Richard Marsden was flying over the North Sea in 1992 at a height of 30,000 feet. He was 150 miles east of Newcastle, flying a Tornado aircraft along with a similar aeroplane when they both saw a UFO. After giving chase for several miles they decided to give up, as they were low on fuel.

Over the North Sea on 19 September 1952 two RAF officers and crew from RAF Topcliffe saw a UFO following a Meteor aircraft as it approached RAF Dishforth, North Yorkshire, at 1,000 feet. It was about five miles behind the Meteor aircraft. Flight Lieutenant John Kilburn reported this incident to the head of Project Blue Book, USA, and Captain Edward Ruppelt.

In 1830 strange phenomena occurred in East Anglia, Norfolk, England. Lady Cranworth of Cranworth Manor, Letton, Norfolk, had a servant called Kitty and this extract from the *Eastern Counties Magazine*, 1900, was her account of what happened. Kitty was aged 107 years when she told the story to a village nurse, who was herself seventy-five years old.

I was a servant in the village of Shipham, near Woodford, Norfolk. (England.) I lived as a servant at the old farm yonder, as was Mason's in those days and I was in bed. . . . Then I saw it right plain and no horses to it. . . . I called out to my old missus and she come and she say 'You Kitty get back to bed that's naught the likes of you to be lurking out. . . .' But she lucked till it goes by. . . . Then next morning folks got a talking. . . . Then when it come to turn down to Woodford, opposite to the little gate on that far side of the road, it vanished away. . . .

The noise of the 'cart' was so load as to wake up Kitty. She would never have seen a car or an aircraft in 1830. Therefore we must conclude that either she and all the other witnesses were having a mass delusion, or they all had the same dream, or all saw a ghost, or it was a genuine UFO sighting. If – and I subscribe to this – they did witness a UFO, then it must be one of the very first recorded sightings in that area.

Phantom coaches have been seen all over East Anglia. Kitty was not the only person to hear the 'phantom' coach; several witnesses, who published their stories in local papers, have seen them on the A5. Usually there is no noise; however, in more recent times noises have been recorded.

When Kitty said, "There were no horses," this would have been natural for those times. Usually there are no lights, unlike Kitty's version.

The Lantern Men are a phenomenon that is not only apparent in Norfolk. Again and again we read of scampering little people who disappear. "I seed them scores of times," we read of appearances in many counties, usually in England.

Evidence that they do not want to be caught can be seen in Ireland, where leprechauns, fairies and elves appear and disappear at will. Did, I wonder, Shakespeare know this when he wrote *A Midsummer Night's Dream*?

Old inhabitants of Norfolk will be heard saying, "They run about and they be tiny."

When records disappear we have to wonder why, especially when not only newspapers but also whole libraries are wiped out, supposedly by an accidental fire. Official explanations cannot always be believed.

A fire in the record office at Norwich in the 1990s destroyed some of the newspapers containing these stories and others not recorded elsewhere. The original research for the incident related above came from Alan Murdie, writing in the November 2001 edition of *UFO Magazine*.

In East Anglia at 2.45 a.m. on 26 December 1980 (the same time as the Rendlesham incident) a meteor was seen and reported in this area. Coincidence or another sighting of the alien craft that visited Rendlesham?

Michael Heseltine, MP, the Minister for Defence, was reported to have commented that there had been no cover-up at his ministry over the sightings in both places. Mrs Margaret Thatcher was reported to have stated, "You can't tell the people."

This became the title of a book written by Georgina Bruni, who will be remembered for her research into the Rendlesham Forest incident, for which the Chief of Defence, Lord Hill-Norton, and Gordon Williams, who had been the commanding officer at the Woodbridge and Bentwaters bases at the time of the incident, praised her. The writer and MOD official Nick Pope held her in high esteem. Georgina Bruni was born in 1947 and died on 19 January 2008.

What exactly Mrs Thatcher meant was not clear, but we assume that she was referring to extraterrestrial visits, as this was the topic of conversation.

Ralph Noyes, former undersecretary at the Ministry of Defence headed the investigation into the incident at Rendlesham Forest and his conclusion, it is alleged, was that "We now have the evidence, I blush to say of my own Ministry of Defence, that they have lied about this matter – they have covered it up." (Report taken from *The World's Greatest Atlas*.)

For many years the US Army, and afterwards the CIA, funded a secret programme known as Stargate, which set out to investigate premonitions and the ability of mediums to predict the future. Scientists who worked on the project became convinced that some soldiers had an inbuilt mechanism which allowed them to see the future and make life-saving decisions. Recruits to Stargate were able to describe in detail the Soviet Union's secret missile base, which could not be seen by reconnaissance aircraft or orbiting spy satellites.

During the Second World War an elderly lady 'saw' the sinking of a ship and when she told people she was declared a witch, as the ship didn't sink until the next day.

When the British Government heard the story the lady was thrown into prison as a spy, because the ship had indeed been sunk that day and there had been a cover-up.

Decades after premonition studies were shelved in the sixties, the science is now being revived with experiments conducted at a British university.

Dr Richard Broughton of the University of Northampton says, "Many physicists do not see any problem with the concept of information flowing backwards in time!"

Humans have evolved to be exceptionally good at information processing. We have gone from cave paintings to the Internet in 50,000 years. Who knows where we are going in the future when we are further down the evolutionary path! Dr Broughton suggests that there may be people who already have a psychic ability, but find it difficult to control.

Similar trials are alleged to be taking place at the University of Amsterdam. Professor Dick Bierman, a psychologist, is reputed to have declared that people may be able to sense the future before it happens. It has not yet been conclusively proven what kind of person is most likely to have this latent ability and how best to nurture it has not been established. These two forward thinkers are leaders in their field and it is hoped that in time many more will follow their lead. (From the *Daily Express*, 2007.)

By 2015 the ESA will launch a telescopic craft designed in Darwin, Australia, that will search for Earth-like planets.

According to *UFO Magazine*, 'In America the Code of Federal Regulations states that; FROM July 1969, it is illegal for U.S. citizens to have any contact with Extraterrestrials or their vehicles.'

CHAPTER ELEVEN

RUGBY, A CYCLICAL HOT SPOT

It has been alleged that the Ministry of Defence admitted in 2001 to a local reporter that the Midlands are a cyclical UFO hot spot. (*UFO Magazine*, 2002.)

Mr W. J. Clarke, who lived in Rugby, found a live toad in a piece of coal. Imagine his surprise to find that the living toad had no mouth or rectum! The creature could have been thousands of years old and yet still lived and breathed. Mr Clarke reported this find to the local newspapers and it was said to live for a further five weeks before taking its last breath. (From *The World's Greatest Mysteries*.)

In 1973 the M1 between Northamptonshire and Nottingham was blocked on 31 October by a terrible storm causing trees to fall. Visibility was almost nil, and vehicles were forced to take the back roads. The A60, A6 and A50 south of Leicester were used while the storm blew itself out. Mr Ron Stone stopped his car to ask the way when he saw two tall men. They were over six feet tall and dressed all in black. Their suits had a hood below long necks. They had small bald heads; their eyes were large, black and luminous. As Mr Stone approached them they got into their car and shot away at great speed.

Mr Ian Morrison, director of Jodrell Bank, on Wednesday

23 January 2002 was asked for his opinion on the transmissions that were re-entering the Earth's atmosphere in Daventry. Mr Morrison denied any knowledge of the transmissions. However, a Mr Roy Chandler, who lived in Australia during the Second World War, had personal experience of the returned messages. He wrote an article to the effect that when he swore at a colleague using coarse language this message reappeared months later. He said that it was definitely himself on the re-entering message. Maybe it had bounced off a satellite? I believe there were none in 1944. Roy Chandler believed that some form of extraterrestrial might have bounced back the transmission to get our attention. This does seem to give credence to the Daventry incident. Daventry radio masts were dismantled many years ago – apparently they were no longer needed, as they were not as powerful as the Rugby ones. The Borough Hill site in Daventry still has an underground facility guarded by a very high fence. During the Second World War the French Resistance used code words when communicating with Rugby Radio Station and these codes appear to be similar to the ones 'echoing' back to Daventry Radio Station a few miles away. "Daffodils coming up early this year," for example. Naturally Jodrell Bank denied any knowledge of this as they were probably not aware of the messages in the first place. Certain people have been directed to say that it was all a hoax and that the echoes did not return. Well, they would, wouldn't they?

When Pete Chambers wrote his book about the Rugby radio masts, he might have stirred up a hornets' nest when he detailed the code words used from Rugby to the French underground during the Second World War. He also reminds us how easy it was to send messages, authorised by Margaret Thatcher, for the eventual sinking of the Belgrano warship during the Falklands War, from Rugby Radio Station. How much easier it would be for advanced aliens to tap into our wavelengths and return the signals. Naturally these things have to be denied for reasons of national security.

In mid November 1999, Mr Mark Hulcombe was travelling towards Crick, Northamptonshire, when he saw a flying triangle that was hovering some thirty feet above the Rugby radio masts. His report appeared in a guide to the Rugby radio masts, written by Pete Chambers. The book is a fascinating guide and reveals how between 1961 and 1963 NASA used GBR Rugby to assist with the Mercury programme.

High-frequency transmissions from the Rugby radio masts were also used in the Gemini programme and were linked to the top-secret NSA (National Security Agency) listening station at RAF Menwith Hill, North Yorkshire. Pete Chambers claims in the book that BT (British Telecom) is actually controlled by the Ministry of Defence.

During the First World War, the area now housing the masts was an airfield. In 1929 GBR Rugby sent a message to Mars. No reply yet, which is not surprising when you read the message: 'OSIRIS AMVBIS FACE TEN EIGHT FIFTEEN THIRTY-ONE JAXON'.

The Daventry masts have been dismantled and there are now only four at Rugby. These disappeared in August 2007. As the VVVGBR at Rugby was forty times more powerful than those at Daventry it seems such a waste to have them destroyed. There must be more to this destruction than is known to the general public. This facility remains under guard with perimeter fences and tight security. A new Area 51?

Graham Birdsall was extremely interested in this article and publicly congratulated my record keeping (*UFO Magazine*, July 2003.) He was extremely interested in these phenomena and called Rugby a cyclical hot spot on a par with Bonnybridge, Scotland.

In 2008 Dr Edgar Mitchell, a respected scientist and astronaut, is alleged to have admitted that UFOs have visited the Earth and still do. NASA, of course, covers this up for reasons of national security. During his interview with Kerrang! Radio, Dr Mitchell is alleged to have said, "The extraterrestrials are very small beings." He was a crew member on *Apollo 14* with Alan Shepard during their 1971 mission to the moon. He also claimed that life exists all over the universe. For over sixty years this was all kept secret; now some information is being shared. Dr Mitchell is a doctor of science in aeronautical engineering and an astronaut. Does NASA deny these visitations so as not to cause unnecessary panic among the general public?

In 1976 at Moreton Morrell College, Warwickshire, a UFO was witnessed by Nik Bradley and fellow agricultural students. It hovered and travelled up and down an electrical pylon before shooting away suddenly. This is identical to the behaviour my husband and I witnessed at the Rugby radio masts on the A428 junction with the A5 (Watling Street) near the Halfway House public house.

On 29 May 1978 at 2 a.m. several local people, including night workers changing shifts and a policeman, saw a UFO clearly at precisely the same time from different locations around the Rugby and Coventry districts. Scientists speaking on the radio blamed 'the Meaner vortex' for the simultaneous sightings.

As previously mentioned, Georgina Lawry saw a UFO on 22 November 1978 on the day Elsie Oakensen was abducted by a UFO near Stowe Nine Churches, Northamptonshire. In the same county that year UFOs were seen at Nether Heyford, Weedon, Silverstone, Upper Stowe and Dodford. One was also seen between Hillmorton, Warwickshire, and Crick, Northamptonshire, and on 24 November Walter Green, editor of the *Daventry Express* newspaper saw a UFO at Daventry, Northamptonshire.

On 19 June 1997 several people saw a UFO near Dunchurch, Warwickshire, and on the same day at Churchover, also in Warwickshire, a crop circle appeared near to the M6 just outside Rugby, not far from the radio station. On 3 October 1994 on the A5 between Daventry and Kilsby, Northamptonshire, at about 7.30 p.m. our car lights failed, the engine stopped and we lost time (see Chapter Seven) and in 1982 at Corby, Northamptonshire, Miss Ross Reynolds was driving her car when her engine stopped dead. This is almost identical to our own experience on the A5.

In Dartford, Kent, Maria Ward was abducted on 21 November 1990 and the following day at Hillmorton, between Rugby and Crick, a triangle hovered above the Rugby radio masts on the A428 and was seen by John and myself from our car.

On 9 December 1991 all over the Midlands lights were seen in the sky, moving and stationary.

Denis Plunkett, founder and chairman of the British Flying Saucer Bureau, Bristol, wrote:

> I can fully subscribe to the interest shown in the UFO's in the Rugby, Warwickshire area. I was stationed there in 1953/4 at RAF Church Lawford. On two separate occasions I was just a few miles outside the town when I saw UFO's. Maybe the same one that Miss Herbert and the three elderly ladies saw near the Bucknill's lane, at Crick village, Northamptonshire, roughly ten miles away.

He continued to describe a dark sphere that hovered from low cloud in daylight and hovered over a runway at the Church Lawford airbase. During a second encounter, also in daylight, a light flew north to south at a fast speed. His reported sightings are all the more credible as he also gave his report to Nick Redfern to be included in his book *A Covert Agenda*. The secrecy order that Denis Plunkett saw at RAF Church Lawford while he was doing national service was titled 'Reports on Aerial Phenomena'. This was 1953/4 and since then other sightings have been reported to Nick Redfern and appear in his books at a later date.

An unusual sighting witnessed by D. P. Plunkett and his wife occurred in 1966 near to the wireless station at Downend near Winterbourne, South Gloucestershire. For sixty minutes both people watched nine objects hover and disappear as suddenly as they appeared.

In the early 1950s airmen were ordered not to discuss sightings of UFOs with the media or the general public. This seemed strange as the whole country had been intrigued by the flying-saucer reports of 1947, only a few years before, and little boys knew about Travis Walton's adventures.

The local inhabitants remembered the sighting of the second UFO seen by Denis Plunkett because the flight pattern was so unusual. They had seen planes during the war going over to bomb Coventry and heard the returning drone of the ones that came back, dropping the last of their bombs on Watford Hill or the allotments near to the railway line. They had seen the sky blacken with British planes going to fight the Hun. But nothing like the acrobatics of this UFO. It travelled from north to south and suddenly turned to the west. The enormous G forces would have squashed a human pilot all over his windscreen – that is if it had a pilot!

The atomic clock beneath the Daventry masts was moved to Cumbria, probably when the last of the masts were secretly dismantled on 31 March 2007. On 19 June 2004 there were still twelve masts that had been built in 1924. The history of the masts is detailed in the book *Something in the Air*, by Pete Chambers. He tells us that the short waves used at Rugby were using only a tenth of the power of the long-wave transmissions. At 200 words a minute the Morse code sent messages to places all over the world and GBR Rugby became famous in the secret world of signals. Parliament directed Head Wrightson & Co. Ltd to build the facility in 1924. It seemed the perfect choice, as the First World War airfield was flat and 350 feet above sea level. Also, the A5, Watling Street, was close by to enable easy transportation of materials and men.

Rugby railway lines were not bombed in the last war because Hitler's one-time girlfriend Unity Mitford was staying (some say hiding) in the Hillmorton area of Rugby in the rectory. She did in fact – and many can testify to this – live there for a long while, using a wheelchair to get about because of her self-inflicted wounds. Maybe the masts were saved for the same reason, being only a mile from the rectory in Hillmorton. The masts are sometimes referred to as Hillmorton masts.

One visitor of note to the station was welcomed on 29 August 1928; it was the Prince of Wales, Edward, who became King Edward III. He climbed the masts in a cage to view the countryside.

NASA in 1961/3 needed help with the Mercury project; this was the first space flight for *Freedom 7*, with astronaut Alan Shepard on board. Later, when America needed assistance with the Gemini project they called on the Rugby Radio Station to help with transmissions. No wonder the masts have been taken down, if extraterrestrials have at last located them after all these years of trying.

Most roads around the Daventry, Rugby, Hillmorton and Crick areas are important for their several sightings by local people and visitors. Most are reluctant to speak publicly of what they have seen. This is understandable as it is only after retirement that I have gained the courage to speak of my experiences to people outside my immediate family.

Do not dismiss the book as entire fiction. All the sightings and information given here either have been published in other works or are the testimonies of reliable people – including my own experiences. The reason for writing this book was to try to get other believers in historical and present-day sightings to speak out.

PEOPLE MUST KNOW THE TRUTH.